DEBUGGING
THE
DEVELOPMENT
PROCESS

DEBUGGING THE DEVELOPMENT PROCESS

Practical Strategies for Staying Focused, Hitting Ship Dates, and Building Solid Teams

STEVE MAGUIRE

Author of *Writing Solid Code*

Microsoft PRESS

PUBLISHED BY
Microsoft Press
A Division of Microsoft Corporation
One Microsoft Way
Redmond, Washington 98052-6399

Library of Congress Cataloging-in-Publication Data
Maguire, Stephen A.
    Debugging the development process : practical strategies for
staying focused, hitting ship dates, and building solid teams /
Stephen A. Maguire
        p.   cm.
    Includes bibliographical references and index.
    ISBN 1-55615-650-2
    1. Debugging in computer science. 2. Computer software-
-Development.   I. Title.
QA76.9.D43M33 1994
005.1'068--dc20   94-22182
                                                             CIP

Printed and bound in the United States of America.

1 2 3 4 5 6 7 8 9   MLML   9 8 7 6 5 4

Distributed to the book trade in Canada by Macmillan of Canada, a division of Canada Publishing Corporation.

A CIP catalogue record for this book is available from the British Library.

Microsoft Press books are available through booksellers and distributors worldwide. For further information about international editions, contact your local Microsoft Corporation office. Or contact Microsoft Press International directly at fax (206) 936-7329.

Apple, Mac, Macintosh, and MultiFinder are registered trademarks of Apple Computer, Inc. Alpha AXP and DEC are trademarks of Digital Equipment Corporation. PC-lint is a trademark of Gimpel Software. HP is a registered trademark of Hewlett-Packard Company. Comdex is a registered trademark of Interface Group-Nevada, Inc. CodeView and Microsoft are registered trademarks and Windows and Windows NT are trademarks of Microsoft Corporation. MIPS is a registered trademark of MIPS Computer Systems, Inc.

Acquisitions Editor: Mike Halvorson
Project Editor: Erin O'Connor
Technical Editor: Wm. Jeff Carey

To my brother Tim.

CONTENTS

If a software project is to be successful, every team member must understand the principles, guidelines, and strategies that will result in quality software shipped on time. This book is for every team member. It's a companion to Writing Solid Code, *which focused on the most serious "bug" in the development process: too many software bugs. The advice in this book fine-tunes the development process, focusing on the techniques and strategies that software teams can use to become consistently successful. This book contains many anecdotal examples, most of them drawn from experiences at Microsoft. To make the examples easier to follow, the introduction provides a brief account of how software development projects are organized and how they proceed at Microsoft.*

1 LAYING THE GROUNDWORK _____ 1

There are a few principles that all successful software project leads keep in mind. Among the foremost is the idea that the programmers should be working only on tasks that either directly or indirectly improve the product. It's the lead's job to clear the way for the primary work of the other team members by ruthlessly eliminating work that gets in the way of improving the product—going overboard on status reports and meetings, for example, or developing features that are not strategic to either the product or the company. To make it easy to determine which tasks are strategic and which are wasted effort, leads should create detailed project goals and priorities. The more detailed the goals and priorities are, the easier it is to spot wasteful work.

2 THE SYSTEMATIC APPROACH _____ 23

It's amazing how a relatively trivial work habit or process can produce a major difference in results. Ideally, the habit or process will take little or no effort to put into practice and its effectiveness won't depend on the skill levels of the programmers who use it. To elicit the best strategies for working effectively, leads should pose the problems they're trying to solve as increasingly refined questions. A lead shouldn't ask, for example, "How can we consistently hit our ship dates?" which can result in a number of undesirable solutions. The lead should instead ask a more specific, more beneficial question: "How can we consistently hit our ship dates without hiring more people and without forcing the developers to work overtime?" Leads should try to incorporate negative feedback loops into the strategies they develop. And when they present work strategies to the rest of the team, they should be sure to remind the team that even a good strategy or guideline won't necessarily be effective in every situation.

3 OF STRATEGIC IMPORTANCE _____ 45

Projects can go astray in so many subtle ways that leads must never let projects coast, assuming that their projects are on course and will run themselves. To keep a project running smoothly, a lead must constantly monitor the project, looking ahead and taking care of problems while they're still small. To keep a project on schedule, a lead should ask this question each day: "What can I do *today* that will help keep the project on track for the next few months?" By asking this question every day and seriously looking for answers, a lead can foresee all sorts of problems that might otherwise blindside the project. To prevent wasted effort, a lead should assess every request in order to identify the real problem or goal and should be sure that every task fulfills the project's goals and priorities. Some tasks, such as meeting the marketing team's request to fill out a feature set, or implementing a free feature that has popped out of a programmer's design, might not be at all strategic. A good lead learns to say No.

4 UNBRIDLED ENTHUSIASM _____ 73

If a lead wants to get a software development team going on a creative roll, he or she must create a development atmosphere that fosters that kind of enthusiasm. Unfortunately, as companies grow from small mom-and-pop shops to corporate mega-shops, the amount of non-development work that programmers are routinely saddled with rises dramatically. The lead should work to eliminate unnecessary reports and meetings and other corporate processes that hinder the development effort. The simpler such processes become, the better. If programmers are given the opportunity to work unhindered by overblown corporate processes, they have a much better chance of catching a creative wave and moving the project forward. The critical point is that leads should always work to address their actual, rather than formal, needs. Asking for a report or holding a meeting is a common way to gather information, but if there are other, more effective ways to gather information (and there are), why burden programmers with reports and meetings?

5 SCHEDULING MADNESS _____ 91

In most companies, the development team needs to maintain a schedule so that other groups in the company can coordinate their work with the programming effort. At the very least, the marketing team needs to have some idea of when they should start advertising the product. But as important as schedules are for coordinating the work of the various product teams, they can have a devastating effect on development if they are not devised and used wisely. An unattainable schedule can demoralize the team and ultimately kill productivity. A schedule that is merely too aggressive can lead to slip hysteria, in which programmers take shortcuts to meet the schedule in the short term, jeopardizing the product over the long term. A schedule should be aggressive enough to keep the project running at a brisk pace, but if it is too aggressive, programmers will make stupid decisions despite their better judgments. Any programmer who has decided that he doesn't have time to thoroughly test his code is guilty of putting the schedule ahead of the product. By using "milestone scheduling," leads can not only coordinate better with other teams but also make projects much more exciting and foster creative rolls in which teams crank out high-quality code at a prodigious rate.

6 CONSTANT, UNCEASING IMPROVEMENT _____ 107

Leads can streamline the development process to a point at which every team member is focused only on strategic work. But if leads want their projects to really take off, they have to focus on training so that every team member is regularly learning a wide variety of broadly useful new skills. One method for ensuring that team members actively grow is to align personal growth goals with the two-month project milestones described in Chapter 5, which could give each team member at least six important new skills a year. Programmers can and do pick up skills in the normal course of the job, but their growth is much slower in that passive approach to learning. By ensuring through work assignments and overt educational goals that programmers actively learn new skills, leads help the project and the company and advance the programmers' careers.

Increasing a team member's skill through active learning is great, but leads can get the most impressive results when they focus on correcting harmful attitudes and promoting beneficial ones. The effects of a new attitude sweep across all work that a programmer will do. That's the leverage behind good attitudes. Chapter 7 takes a hard look at the common programmer attitudes that work to the detriment of project success: bugs are inevitable, I'll fix bugs later, it'll take too much time to do things right, it's good enough for users, it's better to give the user something than nothing, we'll do our thing and you do yours, it's just for in-house use. . .

When a project schedule starts to slip, a natural reaction is to hire more people and force the team to work longer hours. But throwing more programmers at the project and forcing everybody to work overtime won't correct the underlying problems that caused the project to slip in the first place. If a team is working 80-hour weeks to meet a 40-hour schedule, something is seriously wrong. The lead needs to go after causes and (sometimes) to protect the programmers from assumptions—their own and upper management's—about the tonic effects of long hours. Hiring more people or demanding long hours only masks the problems affecting the project. Leads should find and fix the problems, not cover them over.

PREFACE

This book might make Microsoft sound bad.

At least that's one of the concerns I had about telling so many Microsoft war stories. I considered softening and smoothing over some of the stories, or leaving them out altogether, but apart from changing people's names, I decided to keep this book and its examples grounded in reality so that it would be as useful and practical as possible. Besides, I think people realize that Microsoft wouldn't have reached its position of prominence in the software industry if the company were full of bozos. It isn't.

Most of the incidents I describe come from my experiences in retraining Microsoft teams whose projects were already in some sort of trouble: the projects were long overdue, or the quality of the code was not up to the company's standards, or the programmers were working crazy hours and still not making any headway. . .

While working with these teams, I discovered that they were all making the same fundamental errors and that they were perpetually repeating those errors. Not only that, once I'd gotten attuned to the mistakes those teams were making, I saw that even teams on successful projects were making those same fundamental errors—they just made the mistakes less often or had instituted countermeasures to overcome the effects of those mistakes.

In every group I worked with, I found that the project leads were spending nearly all of their time writing code and almost none of their time thinking about the project. The leads didn't spend time trying to keep schedules on track, they didn't look for foreseeable problems so that they could circumvent them, they didn't work to protect other team members from unnecessary work, they didn't pay particular attention to training other team members, and they didn't set detailed project goals or create effective attack plans. The leads were spending too much time *working* when they should have been *thinking*.

In many ways, this state of affairs wasn't really the fault of the leads. The leads hadn't been trained to be leads. They were programmers who woke up one day to find themselves, for one reason or another, plunked into lead positions. These new leads knew how to program well, but they didn't know how to run projects well, so they focused on what they knew best and allowed their projects to run themselves—right into the ground.

Unfortunately, many programmers don't feel that they need to know how to lead a project: "I'm not a lead, so why should I worry about lead issues?" They seem to think that once they become leads they'll have time then to learn what they need to do in order to run a project effectively. That's a little late.

I wrote this book's companion, *Writing Solid Code*, to give programmers proven techniques and strategies they could use to immediately start writing code with far fewer bugs than they currently do. I've written *Debugging the Development Process* to give leads and programmers the proven techniques and strategies they can use to organize and run software projects without the turmoil, long hours, and schedule slips that are so common in our industry.

It *is* possible to ship high-quality, bug-free software on schedule, without working long hours—and to have fun doing it. The techniques and strategies in this book should help you do that.

ACKNOWLEDGMENTS

Many, many people at Microsoft Press worked on this book, and I'm not sure that they, or people at publishing houses anywhere, get enough credit for all the effort they put in behind the scenes when they take a manuscript in hand and deliver it to readers as a book. My thanks first to Mike Halvorson, who believed in this book when it was a mere idea. My thanks in particular to Erin O'Connor, my manuscript editor, who was a joy to work with and who spent nearly a year working with me on the book. This book is as much hers as it is mine. Jeff Carey's enthusiastic responses to the chapters kept me encouraged. Deborah Long's good ear for idiom saved me from myself more times than I care to count, and the other proofreaders/copyeditors on her team—Alice Smith, Therese McRae, and Pat Forgette—kept me busy considering the most fitting way to put things. Compositor Peggy Herman worked patiently and inventively to accommodate revisions in both the text and the layout. Kim Eggleston adapted her fine design for *Writing Solid Code* to serve the purposes of this book and cleverly adjusted the design as new requirements arose. My thanks to all of these professionals and to the many others at Microsoft Press who worked to make this book a reality: Judith Bloch, Wallis Bolz, Barb Runyan, Jeannie McGivern, Sandi Lage, Shawn Peck, John Sugg, Geri Younggren, and Dean Holmes.

I would like to mention two educators who over the years have greatly influenced the way I lead projects. Anthony Robbins conducts seminars to help CEOs and other executives run their businesses more effectively. (Robbins is perhaps better known for his personal achievement seminars, which are also excellent.) Anyone who is familiar with Robbins's work will see his influence in spots throughout this book. Michael E. Gerber speaks to business audiences about how to "bring the dream back to American business" and wrote the book *The E-Myth: Why Most Businesses Don't Work and What to Do About It*. Gerber's ideas, book, and speeches would seem to have nothing do with writing software—they focus on how to run franchise businesses—but many of Gerber's insights completely changed the way I view software projects and how they should be run. My thanks to both of these educators. Information on their companies appears in the "References" section at the end of this book.

I was fortunate to have a wonderful team of programmers and project leads as reviewers of this book. They provided generously from their experience and insight. They are Microsoft programmers and project leads who have worked over the years on Microsoft's most strategic projects. As reviewers they worked to ensure that my advice adequately treated the problems and issues they have encountered on their projects. I thank Paul W. Davis, Melissa Glerum, Eric Schlegel, and Alex Tilles. My special thanks to Dave Moore, who gave of his longtime experiences as a programmer, project lead, director of development, and more recently general manager to help me refine the points in this book. I would also like to thank Ian Cargill for the several important insights he provided early in the writing of the book.

Seattle, Washington
June 21, 1994

INTRODUCTION

Inspiring leaders look at the world in a funny way. The company building could be burning to the ground, and instead of panicking about the lost jobs, the inspiring leader takes one look at the flames and breaks out the hot dogs and marshmallows. When everybody around them is pessimistic, such leaders inspire confidence even though there may be every reason to be pessimistic. They're an optimistic bunch, tending to interpret events in a positive light. With that perspective, inspiring leaders tend to view failures not as failures but merely as learning experiences that will help them surmount the next obstacles that come along. And because inspiring leaders tend not to experience a sense of failure, they're willing to try the outlandish ideas that can lead to major breakthroughs. If an outlandish idea flops, the inspiring leader doesn't see the episode as a failure but merely as more information. Such leadership has little to do with experience. It's a combination of strong desire, an unusual way of looking at the world and its opportunities, and such a clear vision and the ability to communicate that vision that others are inspired to work with the leader to see that the vision comes true.

Despite the belief that such leaders are born and not made, it is possible to learn to be an inspiring leader. It isn't easy, though. Usually the person must change many of his or her fundamental beliefs and attitudes in order to view the world in that peculiar way. You might say that it calls for a personality makeover—an idea that most people would think impossible and that many would find repugnant. I think that's why it's rare for people to become inspiring leaders partway through their lives. People don't usually change their personalities to that extent.

THE REST OF US

Fortunately, most software project leads aren't starting new companies or venturing off into uncharted territory. The typical lead is usually embarking on the development of version 4.21 of an application or working on some other project that has a fairly straightforward future everybody is in basic agreement about. The typical software lead doesn't need to be a radically inspiring leader capable of getting team members to do outlandish things. The typical software lead simply needs to be *effective*, which is quite learnable and doesn't require anything like a personality transformation. It just requires learning the habits and strategies that have been found to work in bringing quality products to market on schedule—and without working 80-hour weeks.

All effective leads understand that for a project to be successful, every single member of the team must be in on the strategies that will be used to ship a quality product on schedule. You don't have to be the lead in order to make good use of the techniques and strategies I describe. This book is for every team member, not just the lead. Unless every team member knows what it takes to get a quality product out the door without working 80-hour weeks, it won't happen.

WRITING SOLID CODE

A lot of steps are involved in the development team's effort to bring a software product to market—everything from designing the code to working with the marketing team. In every one of the steps in the development process, people make mistakes. There's nothing new in that observation. I've called this book *Debugging the Development Process* to get programmers to think of the development process as they would a coding algorithm: it's something that can contain bugs that will cause wasted and misguided effort, and it's something that can be optimized to function better.

In *Writing Solid Code*, the companion book to this one, I focused on what I believe is the most serious "bug" in the development process: that there are far too many programming bugs. *Writing Solid Code* described the techniques and strategies programmers can use to detect existing bugs at the earliest possible moment and how programmers can prevent those bugs in the first place.

In *Debugging the Development Process*, I focus on the techniques and strategies that programmers can use to get quality products out the door with a minimum of wasted effort. In the first three chapters, I talk about a number of basic concepts and strategies that a team should act on if they want to release products without working twelve hours a day, seven days a week. The final five chapters build on the earlier chapters, focusing singly on overblown corporate processes, the ins and outs of scheduling, programmer training, attitudes, and long hours.

Writing Solid Code and *Debugging the Development Process* are companion books. You'll find that the ideas in the two books interact with one another to a certain extent. When ideas in the two books overlap, you'll find that *Writing Solid Code* tends to be more focused on the code itself. In one instance I excerpt part of a section from *Writing Solid Code* in this book because I think that the point it makes is even more critical to the smooth running of a project than it is to writing bug-free code.

DEVELOPMENT AT MICROSOFT—A SNAPSHOT

Most of the examples in this book are drawn from my experience at Microsoft. A brief description of how responsibilities are divided among leads and a sketch of how a typical project proceeds at Microsoft might put those examples in context for you.

A Microsoft project typically has at least three different types of leads working directly on the development of the product:

◆ Project Lead. The project lead is ultimately responsible for the code. He or she is also responsible for developing and monitoring the schedule, keeping the project on track, training the programmers, conducting program reviews for upper management, and so on. The project lead is usually one of the most experienced programmers on the team and will often write code, but only as a secondary activity.

◆ Technical Lead. The technical lead is the programmer on the team who knows the product's code better than anyone else. The technical lead is responsible for the internal integrity of the product, seeing that all new features are designed with the existing code in mind. He or she is also usually responsible for ensuring that all technical documents for the project are kept up-to-date: file format documents, internal design documents, and so on. Like the project lead, the technical lead is usually one of the most experienced programmers on the project.

◆   Program Manager. The program manager is responsible for coordinating product development with marketing, documentation, testing, and product support. In short, the program manager's job is to see that the product—everything that goes into the box—gets done, and that it gets done at the level of quality expected by the company. The program manager usually works with the product support team to coordinate external beta releases of the product and works with end users to see how the product might be improved. Program managers are often programmers themselves, but they limit their programming to using the product's macro language (if one exists) to write "wizards" and other useful end user macros. More than anyone else, the program manager is responsible for the "vision" of what the product should be.

The name "program manager" can be misleading because it implies that the program manager is superior in rank to the project lead, the test lead, the documentation lead, and the marketing lead. In fact, the program manager is at the same level as the other leads. A more appropriate name for the program manager would be "product lead" since the program manager is responsible for ensuring that all the parts of the product—not just the code—get done on schedule and at an acceptable level of quality.

On a typical project, the program manager (or managers if the project is large enough) works up front with the marketing, development, and product support teams to come up with a list of improvements for the product. After the list of features has been created, the program manager writes the product specification, which describes in detail how each feature will appear to the user—providing, for instance, a drawing of a new dialog box with a description of how it will work, or the name of a new macro function with a description of its arguments. As soon as the product spec has been drafted, it is passed out to all of the teams involved with the product for a thorough review. Once the final spec has been nailed down, the teams go to work.

The program manager meanwhile uses mock-ups of features to conduct usability studies to be sure that all of the new features are as intuitively easy to use as everybody originally thought they would be. If a feature turns out to be awkward to use, the program manager proposes changes to the spec. The program manager also works on sample documents for the product disks and on those end user macros I mentioned earlier. As features are completed, he or she reviews each to ensure that it meets all the quality standards for shipping the product—in particular, that the feature is snappy enough on low-end machines.

Development continues and eventually reaches a point known as "visual freeze," meaning that all features that will affect the display have been completed. Once the code reaches the visual freeze point, the user manuals are finalized with screen shots of the program. Consequently, from that point on, developers have to be careful not to affect the display in any way so that the screen shots in the manuals won't differ from what the user sees in the program. The programmers, of course, would prefer that the screen shots be taken only after all the code is finished, but the manuals need a long lead time and have to be sent to the printer well before the code will be finalized. In some cases, in order to reach visual freeze on all the features in time for the manuals to be ready at the release date, the programmers will only partially implement the features—for instance, displaying a nonfunctional dialog good for screen shots but not much else. The programmers come back to the features and fully implement them later.

Once all of the features have been completed—the "code complete" stage—the programmers put their effort into fixing all outstanding bugs in the bug-list and making any necessary performance improvements. When the code is finally ready to be shipped, the project lead or the technical lead creates the "golden master disks." The program manager sends the golden masters off to manufacturing for duplication, and the software gets stuffed into the boxes with the manuals, the registration cards, and other goodies. A little bit of shrink-wrap, and the product is ready for an end user.

I've left out a lot of details, but this brief overview should be enough to enable you to put the occasional example in this book that might otherwise be too Microsoft-specific into context.

I should also mention that e-mail is the lifeblood of Microsoft. All internal business is conducted over e-mail, and, at least in development circles, you have to have a really good reason to interrupt someone with a telephone call. Most interaction among developers goes on over e-mail and in the numerous hall meetings that spring up spontaneously. This corporate sensitivity to interruptions accounts for Microsoft's policy of giving everyone a private office with a door. If you're working and you don't want to be interrupted, you simply close your door.

IT'S HARDER THAN IT SOUNDS

My final concern is that this book might make it sound as if applying all of its advice will, overnight, transform a less-than-model project. Certainly you can apply many of its techniques and strategies immediately, and you will get quick results; but others—some of the training techniques, for instance—take time to produce results. If your team is currently having trouble, you can't expect to read this book and a week later have your project turned around. In my experience, turning around a troubled project takes two to six months, with most of the improvement coming about in those first two months. From that point on, the improvements come more slowly and are less dramatic.

1

LAYING THE GROUNDWORK

Have you ever stopped to consider what makes one project lead or programmer more effective than another? Is it one or two profound pieces of wisdom, or is it a grab bag full of little snippets of knowledge that when taken together produce this thing we call "mastery"?

I wish the answer were that mastery comes from just one or two profound insights—that would certainly simplify training. The reality is that mastery is a collection of numerous little bits of knowledge, beliefs, skills, and habits that beginners have yet to accumulate. Ironically, none, or at least very few, of these little bits of experience are particularly hard to come by. But there are a lot of them, and they are often learned inefficiently, through trial and error.

Trial and error is the time-honored approach to gaining mastery, but that can be a long, arduous undertaking, even if you dramatically speed the process through active study. A much faster method of jump-starting your skills is to take on the beliefs and habits of people who already excel in your area of interest. They've already learned what you want to know, so why go through all the trouble yourself when you can look at their practices, mimic them, and get similar results?

In this first chapter, I will describe what I have found to be the most important practices that project leads and their team members should embrace if they want to stay focused and hit their ship dates without having to work 80-hour weeks. These points lay the groundwork for the following chapters.

FOCUS ON IMPROVING THE PRODUCT

Companies pay programmers to produce useful, high-quality products in a reasonable time frame. But programmers often get sidetracked into doing work that has nothing to do with creating a product. They, or their leads, fail to recognize a basic truth of product development:

Any work that does not result in an improved product is potentially wasted or misguided effort.

If you don't immediately see why this point is so important, consider two extremes. Which programmer is more likely to produce a useful, high-quality product in a reasonable time frame: the programmer who regularly attends meetings, writes status reports, and is buried in e-mail or the programmer who uses all her time to research, design, implement, and test new features? Is there any question that the first programmer's schedule will slip whereas the second, much more focused, programmer not only is likely to finish on schedule but may even finish early?

I've found that groups regularly get into trouble because programmers are doing work they shouldn't be doing. They're spending too much time preparing for meetings, going to meetings, summarizing meetings, writing status reports, and answering e-mail. Some programmers initiate this kind of activity themselves. More often, such distractions are at the behest of a misguided lead.

One lead with whom I worked required every team member to send a weekly e-mail message reporting on the status of his or her work. The entire team would then meet for an hour or so to rehash what everybody had been doing and to discuss any external issues that had cropped up. After the meeting, anybody who had offered new information would have to write those thoughts down in another piece of e-mail and send it off to the lead.

Now, this lead was just trying to be thorough. What he didn't realize was that he was choking his team with a lot of pointless process work. Was it really necessary to have both status reports and status meetings? And what about those follow-up reports? Were they really necessary, or could they have been eliminated in 99 percent of the cases if the lead had simply taken better notes during meetings?

Obviously, your answers to such questions will depend on your particular corporate environment, but in the actual case I've just described, the only process work that ever turned out to have any value was the initial status report. I don't remember a single status meeting that was worth the time it took to attend, and every time the lead asked for follow-up reports I winced, thinking, "Why? They just told you what they thought."

I was only an occasional visitor to these regular status meetings, so I wasn't often affected by the status work. I always wondered, though, how much other unnecessary process work that group was routinely saddled with.

In his well-intentioned zeal to be thorough, that group's lead violated what I consider to be a fundamental guideline for project leads:

> *The project lead should ruthlessly eliminate any obstacles that keep the developers from the truly important work: improving the product.*

There's nothing earth-shattering about this observation, yet how many leads do you know who make it a priority to actively look for and eliminate unnecessary obstacles?

If the lead I've been talking about had been actively trying to eliminate unnecessary work, I'm sure he could have come up with a much simpler and more effective method of determining the state of his project. Having status reports, status meetings, *and* follow-up reports was overkill.

———◆———

*Don't waste the developers' time
on work that does not improve
the product.*

———◆———

Don't Take Me Too Literally. . .

When I say that developers shouldn't do any work that doesn't improve the product, don't take that imperative so literally that you keep them from doing their design and testing work and from getting the training they need. None of these activities contributes directly to a single line of code, but they all influence the quality of the products you release. If a developer thinks through and tosses out three flawed designs, for instance, that's far better for the product than having her implement the first design she comes up with.

And team interaction might not have much to do with improving the product, but getting the team together under pleasant circumstances can do a lot to improve morale and ultimately the quality and efficiency of the team's work.

RUN INTERFERENCE

In your own groups, if you want to consistently hit your deadlines, you must protect your development team from unnecessary work. In particular, any time you find yourself about to delegate work to the entire team, stop and ask whether you can protect the team by doing the work yourself. If you have to present a project review to the folks upstairs, for example, is it really necessary to bring development to a halt and require that every programmer write a report summarizing what he or she has done? Not in my opinion. As the lead, you should be able to compile that information without help, and you can then present the information more effectively since it's coming from one source. Yes, it might cost you a couple of hours of your own time, but that's better than disrupting the entire team for a task that does nothing to improve the product.

I often go a step further. If I find that a programmer is getting bogged down in a task that is necessary but that does not improve the product, I will take that task from the programmer, if I can, so that he or she can stay focused. There's no reason—except perhaps for training purposes—for programmers to answer project e-mail questions if they're questions the lead can field. Nor should programmers be attending meetings or writing reports the lead can handle, or better, eliminate altogether.

I know this advice contradicts what many management courses and books have to say about delegating work. I'm not saying that those courses and books are wrong, but you must be smart, that is, selective, about the tasks you delegate. If you're delegating work just to lighten your own load, you're probably hindering the development team with work that does not improve the product. Just because the other team members *can* do the work doesn't mean they *should* do the work.

Have you ever seen a house being moved across town? I don't mean the contents. I mean the house itself—pulled off its foundation and shifted to a large flatbed truck trailer. I like to think of projects as those houses in transit, and of the leads as the people who drive ahead, arranging to have overhead power lines disconnected and removing other obstacles that would block progress. These "leads" make it possible for the house to roll steadily toward its destination, not having to stop along the way.

While the house is rolling, the leads don't expect the truck drivers to pull over at every intersection to help the public utility people disconnect and reconnect the hanging stoplights. Nor do they ask the drivers to stop at tollbooths along the way, or to stop for meetings with the public utility folks who are moving the power lines.

Those "house leads" understand something that many software leads don't: if you want your project to move forward unimpeded, you must actively search out and eliminate all obstacles to progress. Sure, the driver could pull over and pay the toll-taker—he is, after all, the one driving the truck. But doesn't it make more sense for the lead to take care of that task so that progress can continue unabated? Unfortunately, too many software leads delegate when they shouldn't, making their developers do the equivalent of negotiating with the public utility folks and pulling over to deal with the toll-takers. Their projects get slowed—or stopped—by every obstacle that comes along.

———◆———

Shield the development team
from any work that interferes
with progress.

———◆———

But I Lead Other Leads

I've been assuming that you lead programmers; but if you lead testers, documentation writers, or some other type of team, your job is only slightly different from the one I've been talking about. The general idea is that you should make it possible for the members of your team to stay focused on their jobs, whether they're programming, testing code, or writing the manuals.

Even if your team is composed entirely of other leads, you should determine what their jobs should be and protect them from unnecessary distractions. Holding status meetings for leads can be just as wasteful as holding status meetings for programmers, particularly if the leads work on independent projects and don't need to know the status of other groups' projects. You may not be pulling those leads from the important work of directly improving their products, but in such cases you are pulling them from the important work of clearing obstacles to the improvement of their projects.

THERE'S ALWAYS A BETTER WAY

As a lead, I'm always asking myself one question, in all phases of the project:

What am I ultimately trying to accomplish?

I constantly ask this question because it's so easy to get sidetracked on work that isn't important. If you've ever spent more time formatting a memo—playing with fonts and styles—than you did writing the memo in the first place, you know what I mean. In the moment, you get caught up because the work seems important, but if you step back and get some perspective, you see that it's the message that's important, not how artistic you can make it.

We've already seen an example of misdirected effort in the status meetings and status reports I've talked about. How would you answer this question:

What am I ultimately trying to accomplish by holding status meetings and requiring status reports?

Isn't the primary goal of gathering project status information to detect, at the earliest possible moment, whether the project is going astray? Think about that. Suppose all projects were finished exactly as scheduled—no project end date ever slipped, and nobody ever worked overtime. Would anybody ever gather status information? Of course not. There'd be no reason to.

If the ultimate purpose of status meetings and status reports is to determine whether a project's schedule is in danger of slipping, is it really necessary to pull the development team away from their work to collect this information? I don't think so. I have never held status meetings, and they are the first bit of pointless process I eliminate whenever I become the new lead of a group. I simply don't believe it's necessary to hold status meetings to determine whether a schedule is going to slip—that is, not if you're also collecting status reports.

So what about those status reports? How important are they? I think status reports—of some sort—are a necessary evil. A lead does, after all, need to know when problems occur. But note that while status reports are necessary, they—like status meetings—do not improve the product in any way. When you believe that a task is necessary but see that it doesn't improve the product, you should always ask a more specific form of this general question:

How can I keep the benefits of this task yet remove the drawbacks?

Status reports do serve a valuable purpose, but they take time to write and can create a negative mind set in the team—at least they can the way they have been done in many Microsoft groups.

If each week programmers must write a report accounting for the hours they've worked and explaining why any tasks took more time than originally estimated, the status report causes unnecessary stress and engenders in the developers and everybody else the feeling that the

---

"Status Meeting" Defined

No doubt, what I've been calling a status meeting is going to differ from one company to the next. When I say "status meeting," I mean those dreary get-togethers in which each team member describes what he or she did and didn't do that week. You can spot these meetings easily because the major point is to talk about what did and didn't get done.

Another type of status meeting is one in which leads from different teams get together and describe what they did and didn't get done. Although similar to the project status meeting, these meetings are held to coordinate multi-team projects. The leads don't report every little thing that happened—they report only those items that affect the other groups in the project. Did they miss or make a drop date? Are they still on track for some future date? Is another group now making demands on their time? The purpose of these meetings is to resolve *dependency* issues. Any team that is dependent on another team is in a precarious position as far as its own schedule is concerned, and it's essential that members know, at the earliest possible moment, when a team they're relying on is going to slip a schedule, cut features, or otherwise threaten their own project.

But again, notice that it's the leads who are meeting—not the programmers, who should be off working on their respective projects.

---

project is always slipping. More often than not, a programmer sits down to write the status report and realizes that she can account for only 27 hours of scheduled work yet knows that she worked seven 12-hour days that week. And she knows that she wasn't goofing off all that time.

If you've never been in this position, imagine how frustrating it would be to realize you've slipped your schedule even after you've put in a seven-day week, not to mention that you have to somehow account for your time. And suppose that the same scenario repeats itself week after week. Are you going to jump out of bed each morning, enthusiastic and ready to start another productive day? Or—more likely—are you going to be exasperated, frustrated, and depressed? Each week you work harder, trying to get more work done, yet you continue to slip. . .

I hate such status reports because they force the development team to focus on all the work they *didn't* do instead of putting the emphasis on what they *did* do. Rather than feeling enthusiastic because they are steadily improving the product, the team members are forced to remind themselves that they're behind schedule, screwing up in some way they can't immediately see. They know they're working hard, but they can't seem to keep from slipping.

A team isn't that different from an individual. If a team sees itself as on a roll, it will tend to keep rolling, but if a team sees itself as constantly slipping, the laws of inertia and self-fulfilling prophecy will apply there too, and that is ultimately demoralizing.

Don't misunderstand me: something is definitely wrong if a programmer is working 84-hour weeks but can account for only 27 hours of scheduled work. Perhaps she's agreeing to interview too many job candidates, or attending too many unnecessary meetings, or possibly she's too concerned about how her e-mail reads, so that she edits and re-edits replies that aren't really worth spending that kind of time on. You and she need to address those problems. But even if the programmer is having trouble allocating her time, that's no reason to have the status report regularly slap her in the face. As we'll see later, there are better ways to handle such problems.

Let's return to the earlier question: how can you keep the benefits of having status reports yet remove the drawbacks? One answer is to create a new type of status report, one that takes little or no time to put together and that also makes doing such a report a positive experience rather than a negative one. I'm sure there are many alternative ways of achieving these goals, but this is what I ask my teams to do:

◆ Each time a team member merges a new feature into the master sources, he or she is to send a short piece of e-mail announcing the new functionality to the rest of the team.

◆ Anytime there's a possibility that a feature will slip, the team member responsible for that feature is to drop by my office to discuss the cause and brainstorm a solution.

That's it. A typical status report might look like this:

```
I just checked in the new search and replace feature.
It stomps on the S&R feature in FaxMangler! Check it out.
    - Hubie
```

Imagine how the team members would feel if they were constantly sending and receiving such positive e-mail. Quite a bit different than the hated status reports I talked about earlier would make them feel. Programmers actually enjoy sending little notes like this one—and nobody thinks of such a note as a status report.

When a programmer thinks the feature he or she is responsible for might slip, we talk about the cause and how it can be prevented in the future. Did we forget to schedule time for an important side item? Was the schedule too ambitious? Is a bug somewhere else in the product making this feature difficult to implement or test? Whatever the problem, we try to find some way to prevent it from recurring in the future.

The point is that I can easily gauge the project status solely on the basis of these two kinds of feedback. And if I have to, I can easily pass project status news up the chain of command—the individual programmers don't need to participate in that chore at all.

Even better, both types of feedback have secondary benefits. The first kind reinforces the perception among the team members that the project is continually improving, and the second creates a learning experience for the programmer and the lead. We don't just shrug and say, "Oh well, schedules slip all the time. It's no big deal."

Going overboard in gathering status information is just one example of how process work tends to expand and get formalized into grandiose procedures if people forget what they are really trying to accomplish. They get caught up in the process instead of the product.

Only when you're clear about what you and your team should be doing can you fulfill the project's needs with the least amount of effort and frustration. Review any task assignments that either are unpleasant or pull programmers from working on the product. Can you eliminate the unpleasant tasks, or at least find more enjoyable approaches to accomplishing them? And what about those tasks that don't contribute to improving the product? Get rid of them too, if you can—at least as far as the programmers are concerned.

————◆————

Always determine what you're trying to accomplish, and then find the most efficient and pleasurable way to have your team do it.

————◆————

Bombarded by Success?

You'd think that if you asked team members to send little "check it out" notes to each other, the entire team would be bombarded by e-mail messages announcing their successes. In practice, the number of messages per day is small. The reason: people don't send these messages to everybody on the whole project, just to the lead and the four or five other programmers who are working on their specific part of the project.

One of the larger Microsoft teams might have 50 programmers, but that large team is typically subdivided into much smaller teams, with no more than 5 or 6 programmers working on any specific piece of the project. Each of these "feature teams" has a well-defined area of responsibility, a lead, and its own schedule. Programmers on feature teams are part of the larger team, of course, but on a day-to-day basis, their true team is the 4 or 5 other programmers with whom they share a common project goal.

In practice, you could be on a 50-person project yet receive only a handful of "check it out" notes on any given day—a steady, but not overwhelming number. Just enough messages to give you a sense of constant progress.

STATE YOUR OBJECTIVES

How many people do you know who woke up one day to find that, miraculously, they had taken just the right courses to obtain a computer science degree? How many people do you know who accidentally packed up their houses and moved to new cities? Pretty silly-sounding. Clearly, people don't get college degrees or move across the country by accident. They plan to do those things. At some point they think, "I'm going to become a computer programmer" or "I'd like to live next door to Disney World." Then they take action to make those things happen.

Unfortunately, the random approach to goal achievement works all too well in many other areas of life. You can find a great job by chance, make a killing in the stock market with a lucky pick, and even, sadly, ship a software product without a goal more concrete than "We have to get WordSmasher finished."

In each of these situations, you can achieve the goal, but the question is, How much time and energy will you waste getting there? Are you more likely to get a great job by bouncing from one company to the next, or would it be more effective to take a day to determine what a great job would have to be like and then interview only at companies with jobs that meet your criteria?

One common trait I found among the half-dozen floundering groups I've worked with was that they all had vague goals. In one case, a group was providing a user interface library to 20 or so other groups at Microsoft. Not only was the group swamped with work, but the groups using the library were complaining about the size and bugginess of the code.

After the lead and I reviewed the library's task list, I asked the lead what his goals for the project were.

"To provide a Windows-like user interface library for the MS-DOS character-based applications," he said.

I asked him what else.

"What do you mean?"

"'Providing a Windows-like user interface library' is a pretty vague goal," I said. "Do you have more concrete goals than that?"

"Well, the library should be bug-free."

I nodded. "Anything else?"

He paused a moment and then shrugged. "Not that I can think of."

I then pointed out that a primary goal for any library is to contain only code that will be useful to all the groups using that library. The lead thought that point was obvious, but I wasn't so sure as we began to review the list of features he had agreed to implement.

I pointed to an unusual item near the top of the list. "What's this for?"

"The Works group asked for that. It allows them to. . . ." he said.

"Is it useful to any other group?"

"No. Just the Works group."

I pointed to the next item. "What about this feature?"

"That's for the CodeView team."

"And this item here?"

"Word wants that."

. . .

As we went down the task list, it became clear that the lead had agreed to implement every request that came in. He may have known that a library should contain only code that will be useful to all groups, but he wasn't using that criterion in his decision-making process.

The lead's goal for the library was simply "to provide a Windows-like user interface library." What if his goal had been a bit more detailed?

Goal: To provide a Windows-like user interface library that contains only functionality that is useful to all the groups who will use the library.

With this slightly more precise goal, the lead would have seen that many of the requests from individual groups were inappropriate for a shared library.

After we reviewed the task list, I moved to another problem.

"Many of the groups are complaining that they have trouble linking whenever you release an updated library. What's causing that problem?"

"Oh, that's easy. They're forgetting to change the names of the functions in their source code."

I was confused, so I asked him to show me an example. In one case, he (or another programmer on the team) had fixed a bug in a function, and while he was at it, had changed the function's name so that it was more consistent with the names of other entry points. In another case, a programmer had implemented a new function similar to an existing one. The programmer had then renamed the original function to emphasize the difference between it and the new function.

The lead didn't understand why the other groups were fussing—changing a name is simple. He had never stopped to consider that every time his group changed a name in the library, the 20 or so other groups that used the library would have to search through all their files, changing the names at all the call sites. The lead also hadn't realized that link problems reflected poorly on the library. If the team couldn't do something as simple as release a library that consistently linked, what, the other groups and I had to wonder, must their code be like?

If that lead had spent a moment looking at the library from the other groups' points of view, he would have seen that backward compatibility was important. Groups want to be able to take a new library, copy it to their project, and link. They don't want unexpected errors.

Again, a more concrete set of project goals could have prevented this link problem:

> *Goals: To provide a Windows-like user interface library that*
> *contains only functionality that is useful to all the groups who*
> *will use the library and that is backwards compatible with previous*
> *releases. . .*

Once I understood the issues affecting the user interface library, the lead and I worked out a complete set of goals. What's important to note is that all of the details were apparent, once looked for, and could have been established in advance. If the lead had bothered to ask the question "What am I trying to accomplish with this user interface library?" he could have derived a list of project goals in a matter of minutes.

A more thorough lead would spend several hours or even several days creating detailed project goals. The goals wouldn't have to be profound; they would just need to be written down and put in plain sight so that they could be a constant guide.

By ensuring that all new code would be useful to all groups, the library lead could have kept the library much smaller, he could have finished important features more quickly, and his team probably wouldn't have had to work 80-hour weeks in a desperate attempt to deliver all the features he had promised. Think about that: just one refinement of the goal, and the course of the project could have been dramatically different.

———◆———

Establish detailed project goals
to prevent wasting time on
inappropriate tasks.

———◆———

Dependent on Dependencies

One of the easiest ways for your project to spin out of control is to have it be too dependent on groups you have no control over. Using shared libraries is strategically important for a number of well-known reasons. But as a lead, you must weigh the benefits of leveraging such code against the drawbacks of not having control over the development effort. To keep the dependencies issue in mind—and in sight—you should make this one of the refinements of your project goals:

Minimize the project's dependencies on other groups.

Considering the damage a late library can do to other groups' schedules, a library lead owes it to his or her "customers" to be up front about the library's schedule and warn dependent groups the moment a slip seems likely.

Similarly, a development team relying on shared libraries should listen to a library lead who says a given request can't be fulfilled by a given date. By badgering library teams into accepting requests they don't think they can fulfill on time, pushy leads create not only dependencies for their projects but risky dependencies at that.

These two points are obvious. But having spent years turning around struggling library groups, I've seen both mistakes far too many times.

MAKE THE EFFORT

Management books often make setting goals sound like some mystical ideology you must simply have faith in: "We don't know exactly why setting goals works, but our studies show conclusively that groups who have concrete, detailed goals consistently outproduce those who don't—by a wide margin."

I don't know why such management books make the effectiveness of goal setting sound so surprising—goals simply help you compose a more vivid picture of what it is you're trying to do. If your goal is merely to buy a house, you're going to look at a lot more houses before finding one you like than if your goal is to get a turn-of-the-century, tricolor Victorian with four bedrooms, two bathrooms, and a statue of St. Francis in the back yard. The more detailed goal makes you more efficient because it allows you to instantly reject anything that doesn't match the picture in your head. Specific project goals work because they help you sift through the daily garbage that gets thrown at a project. They help you stay focused on the strategic aspects of your project.

Unfortunately, there's nothing in the software development process that forces project leads to stop and come up with detailed goals. In fact, there's plenty of pressure to skip the whole goal-setting process. Who has time to set goals when a project is out of control from the outset and already slipping like crazy? And some leads skip goal-setting for an entirely different reason: nobody else sets goals—why should they? Leads who don't set goals for either reason cause themselves, and their team members, a lot of unnecessary frustration.

If you want your group to run smoothly, you must take the time to develop detailed goals. It's usually not fun, but taking a day or two to set goals is a small price to pay for having a focused project. No group should have to work long hours under constant pressure—that's a symptom of unfocused work.

———◆———

Don't skip the goal-setting process simply because you think it would take too much time or because nobody else sets goals. The extra effort you exert up front will more than repay you.

———◆———

Know Your Coding Priorities

If you were to ask three different friends to drop by the supermarket to pick up some asparagus, green beans, and corn, would it surprise you to find that one friend bought canned vegetables because they were the cheapest, another bought frozen vegetables because they were easiest to cook, and the third bought fresh vegetables because they were organically grown and tasted the best? Can you at least imagine such a thing happening?

The three friends buy different types of vegetables for the same reason one programmer will emphasize speed in his code, another will emphasize small size in hers, and a third will emphasize simplicity—their choices differ because their priorities are different.

Suppose your product has to be blindingly fast but the programmers on your team are writing code with simplicity in mind. It's unlikely that those programmers are going to use fancy cache-lookups or other faster yet more complicated algorithms. Suppose that your primary goal is to create a robust application in the shortest time possible but the programmers are following their standard policy of writing highly optimized—and risky—code. Again, their misplaced priorities are going to thwart your goal.

Project goals and coding priorities are not the same thing. Goals and priorities do tend to overlap, mainly because the project goals help define what the coding priorities should be. Here's a good generalization:

◆ Project goals drive the direction of the project.

◆ Coding priorities drive the implementation of the code.

Obviously, if your goal is to create the fastest Mandelbrot plotter on the planet, efficiency is going to be a top coding priority.

Despite the importance of coding priorities, in my experience leads rarely convey their coding priorities to the programmers. Should the programmers focus on speed? On size? On safety? Robustness? Portability? Maintainability? Every programmer has his or her personal views about the importance of one coding priority over another and left to his or her own devices will produce code that reflects those views. It's common for one programmer, left alone, to consistently write code that's clean and maintainable while another team member, left alone, focuses on efficiency even if the result is unreadable spaghetti code filled with obscure micro-optimizations and tons of assembly language.

If you want your team to achieve the project goals as efficiently and precisely as possible, you must establish and promote coding priorities to guide the programmers. At the very least, you should establish a ranking order for these priorities:

◆ Size

◆ Speed

◆ Robustness

◆ Safety

◆ Testability

◆ Maintainability

◆ Simplicity

◆ Reusability

◆ Portability

The only item on this list of priorities that may need some explanation is "safety." If you chose safety as a higher priority than speed, you'd choose one design over another because you'd think you'd be more likely to implement the feature without any bugs. Table-driven code, for example, can be slower than logic-driven code, assuming you're scanning the table and not doing a simple lookup, but table solutions are often much safer to implement than logic-driven solutions. If you chose safety as a higher priority than speed in this hypothetical situation, you'd implement the table solution unless there were overriding concerns.

In addition to ranking coding priorities, you should also establish a quality bar for each priority. If robustness is a high priority for you, how robust should the code be? At the very least, the code should never fail for legal inputs, but what about when the code receives garbage as input? Should the code take extra pains to handle garbage intelligently (trading both size and speed for robustness), should the code use program assertions to check for garbage, or should you let Garbage In, Garbage Out rule? There is no right answer to this question; the answer depends on what you're doing.

An operating system should probably accept garbage without crashing; an application program in which an end user can make mistakes entering data most certainly shouldn't crash. But if you're talking about a function deep in the guts of your program, where the only conceivable way the function could get garbage inputs would be if there were a bug elsewhere in your code, an assertion failure would be more appropriate. In such a case, you might still choose to handle the garbage safely if it didn't cost much extra code.

The point is that you must decide, in advance, what the coding priorities and quality bars will be; otherwise, the team will have to waste time rewriting misconceived or substandard code.

———◆———

*Establish coding priorities and quality
bars to guide the development team.*

———◆———

Safety vs. Portability

In my own priority lists, I usually make safety a higher priority than portability—I'd rather have correct code than portable code. This has led to some confusion because portable code is often seen as the safest code of all. In fact, the two priorities aren't really linked; it just happens that portable code is usually quite safe given the constraints that govern the writing of such code.

When writing C code, programmers commonly write macros that look and behave as though they were functions. The problem is that these "macro functions" can cause subtle bugs if they're not written carefully, and even when they're written carefully, they can cause other bugs if they aren't "called" carefully. The problem is well known among experienced C programmers. Macro functions are beneficial but risky.

You can gain the benefits of macro functions without the risks if you're willing to use the nonstandard *inline* directive found in some C compilers. The only cost is that the *inline* directive is not universally portable. Safety over portability. . .

Snap Decisions

You've probably heard that most extremely successful people have a tendency to make on-the-spot decisions. That may seem contrary to what you'd expect—you'd think that people who make snap decisions would fall flat on their faces most of the time. But the difference between these accomplished people and the average person is that they have concrete goals and clear priorities. If you hand such people a problem or a proposal, they instantly measure it against the goals and priorities etched in their brains, and you get an instant answer. The clarity of their goals and priorities also accounts for the other well-known trait of such people: they rarely change their minds once they've made a decision. Changing their minds would mean betraying what they believe in.

These successful people are not actually making snap decisions—that idea implies that no thought is involved. It's simply that these people know their goals and priorities so well that they don't have to wade through all the possibilities that don't match their criteria. The result: they spend their time acting on their decisions, not deliberating over them.

STICK TO THE BASICS

If you look back at the points raised in this chapter, you'll see that they boil down to a simple formula for software development: figure out what you're trying to do and how you should do it, and then make sure that every team member stays focused on the project goals, coding priorities, and quality bars you've come up with. Pretty basic stuff.

Now take a look at the teams in your company. How many have detailed goals for their projects? In how many do the programmers understand exactly how they should be writing their code and to what standards of quality? Then ask yourself, "Are the programming teams focused fully on improving their products?"

Now look at the project leads in your company. Do they habitually call meetings to discuss every little thing, or do they reserve meetings for truly important issues? Do they put obstacles in the programmers'

paths—asking them to write questionably useful reports, for instance—
or do the leads strive to remove obstacles to development work?

The points in this chapter are basic, but in my experience few
groups focus on these fundamental concepts. And that, I believe, is why
you can't pick up *InfoWorld* or *MacWEEK* without reading about some
project that has slipped another six months or on which the programmers are working so hard that they don't even bother to go home
at night.

HIGHLIGHTS

◆ Companies have hired their programmers to focus on creating high-quality products, but programmers can't do that if
they're constantly pulled away to work on peripheral tasks.
Make sure that every team member is focused on strategic
work, not on housekeeping tasks; look for and ruthlessly
eliminate any work that does not improve the product.

◆ Unfortunately, some housekeeping work is necessary, at least
in larger companies. One way to keep such work to a minimum is to regularly ask the questions "What am I ultimately
trying to accomplish?" and "How can I keep the benefits of
the task yet eliminate the drawbacks?" Fulfill the *need*, not
some overblown corporate process.

◆ The benefits of establishing specific goals might not be easy to
see, but it's easy to see the chaos that ensues in groups that
don't set such goals. Yes, creating detailed goals can be tedious; but that up-front work is much less painful than leading a project that slips two days every week. Keep that user
interface library project in mind. One small refinement of the
project goals could have prevented that project from turning
into the pressure cooker it was. A second refinement could
have made it fly.

◆ Every team member needs to know the coding priorities. Is
maintainability important? What about portability? Size?
Speed? If you want the code to reflect the goals for the product, you must tell programmers what trade-offs to make as

they implement features. You must also establish quality bars so that team members won't waste time writing code that will have to be rewritten before you ship. The earlier you define the quality bars, the earlier you'll minimize wasted effort.

2

THE SYSTEMATIC APPROACH

I've been programming computers for almost two decades, so you might be surprised to learn that I don't use a word processor when I sit down to write technical documents or books such as this one. I write everything by hand on a pad of legal paper, and later I transcribe what I've written into a word processor for editing.

I'm obviously not computer-phobic, and writing the old-fashioned way with pen and paper certainly isn't easier than using a word processor. Nevertheless, that's what I do.

I discovered long ago that whenever I sat down to write using a word processor, I would get so caught up in editing every sentence the moment I wrote it that after a day's worth of effort I'd have written almost nothing. Editing was too easy, much easier than writing the next paragraph, and I naturally fell into the habit of doing the easy work. I had to do it sometime anyway, right? In reality, I was editing in order to procrastinate, and it worked all too well.

Once I realized I had been sabotaging my writing effort, I looked for a process I could use to get the results I needed: being able to write technical papers much more speedily. I tried to force myself not to edit as I wrote with the word processor, but I wasn't very successful. I needed a system in which writing would be easier than editing. That's when I stopped using a word processor to write my first drafts and went back to traditional longhand. I now use the word processor only for what it's especially suited for—editing what I've already written.

My new "writing system" solved my procrastination problem by getting me to focus on the writing part of writing.

The important point here is that adopting a trivial process or system can produce dramatic results. I now write five pages in the time it used to take me to write five paragraphs. Was this improvement the result of my becoming a more experienced writer? No. Was it because I worked harder and longer? Again, no. I became a more productive writer because I noticed that the tool I was using had drawbacks and I developed a new system for writing.

As you'll see throughout this chapter, the use of little systems can achieve amazing results. Once you grasp this concept and learn to apply it to your software projects, you can truly claim that you're working smart, not hard, and you can come that much closer to hitting your deadlines without the long hours and daily stress that seem to afflict so many software projects today.

BAD COFFEE

A common problem for servers in coffee shops is remembering who's drinking regular coffee and who's drinking the decaffeinated stuff. A coffee shop manager with unlimited time and resources might send all the servers to Kevin Trudeau's Mega Memory seminar, where they'd learn to vividly imagine a calf with a hide that matches, say, the customer's paisley tie, so that seeing the tie at refill time would trigger the thought of the paisley calf—and de*caf* coffee. Most coffee shop managers take a much simpler approach to the problem, though: they just tell the servers to give you a different kind of cup if you order decaf. The server need only look at your cup to know what type of coffee you're drinking.

A trivial system for solving a common problem.

Now imagine a coffee shop that has a whole collection of such trivial "systems" that produce better results with little or no extra effort. Let's look at another example.

There are two coffee shops near my house. They have identical coffeemakers, they use the same supplier for their beans, and the servers in both places are college students. But one shop consistently brews great coffee, whereas coffee at the other shop is sometimes good, sometimes watery, sometimes too thick, and sometimes burned beyond drinking—you never know what you're going to get when you order coffee there.

Circumstances at the two shops are identical except for one seemingly insignificant detail: the shop that consistently serves great coffee has a short horizontal line embossed on the side of each of its coffee pots. That short line is part of a simple "quality system" that consistently produces good coffee. When a new employee first comes on duty at this shop, the manager pulls him aside and gives him a short lecture:

"Whenever you pour a cup of coffee and the level of coffee drops below this line," he says, pointing to the mark on the pot, "immediately start a new pot. Don't go on to do anything else before you start that new pot."

"What if it's really busy?"

"I don't care if the place is filled with Seattle Seahawks an hour after they've blown a Super Bowl game. Start that new pot before you give Mad Dog Mitchell the cup you've just poured."

The manager goes on to explain that by taking 15 seconds to start a new pot before the old one is empty, the server might make the current customer wait an extra 15 seconds but that the practice prevents the next customer from having to wait a full 7 minutes for a new pot to brew because the current pot ran out.

If you order coffee at the other coffee shop, it's not unusual for the server to reach for the pot only to find it empty, and you have to begin that 7-minute wait. Of course, sometimes you don't have to wait the full 7 minutes. To shorten your wait, some servers will watch until just enough coffee for one cup has brewed and pour you that cup. But for good coffee, you must let the entire pot of water drip through so that the initial sludge can mix with a full pot of hot water. If you pour a cup too early in the process, that cup will be so strong it will be undrinkable, and any other cups you pour from that pot will taste like hot water. That's one reason the quality of the second shop's coffee fluctuates. Depending on when your coffee is poured, you'll get sludge, coffee-colored hot water, or sometimes even normal coffee. And of course occasionally you'll get burned coffee—when the pot holds just enough coffee for one cup and there's not enough liquid to prevent the coffee from burning on the warmer as the water boils out.

The only difference between the two shops is that in one they make coffee when their pots get low and in the other they make coffee when their pots get empty. Their systems are so similar, yet they produce drastically different results, and *the results have nothing to do with the skill of the people involved.*

I wouldn't be talking about these coffee shop systems unless they made a point that related to software development. They do.

If I were to ask you if it mattered when in the software development process your team fixed bugs, provided the bugs were fixed before you shipped the product, what would your answer be? Would you argue that the team shouldn't focus on bugs until all the features have been implemented? Would you argue that bugs should be fixed as soon as they're found? Or would you argue that it doesn't matter, that it takes the same amount of time to fix a bug no matter when you get around to doing it?

If you thought that it doesn't matter when you fix bugs, you would be wrong, just as a coffee shop manager would be wrong if he thought it didn't matter exactly when his servers made new coffee. Possibly the worst position a project lead can find herself in is to be so overwhelmed by bugs that the bugs—not the goals—drive the project. If you want to stay in control of your project, one of your concrete goals must be to never have any outstanding bugs. To ignore this goal is to set a destructive process in motion, one I described in *Writing Solid Code.* There I noted that when I first joined the Microsoft Excel group, it was customary to postpone bug-fixing until the end of the project. I pointed out the many problems that approach created—the worst being the impossibility of predicting when the product would be ready. It was just too hard to estimate the time it would take to fix the bugs that remained at the end of the project, to say nothing of the new bugs programmers would introduce as they fixed old ones. And of course fixing one bug inevitably exposed latent bugs the testing group had been unable to find because the first bug had obscured them.

Concentrating on features and ignoring bugs enabled the team to make the product look much more complete than it actually was. But high-level managers would use the product and wonder why "feature complete" software had to spend six more months in development. The developers frantically debugging the code knew why. Bugs. Everywhere.

When a series of bug-ridden products ended with the cancellation of a buggy unannounced application, Microsoft was finally prompted to do some soul-searching. Here's how I summarized the results of that self-examination in *Writing Solid Code*:

◆ You don't save time by fixing bugs late in the product cycle. In fact, you lose time because it's often harder to fix bugs in code you wrote a year ago than in code you wrote days ago.

◆ Fixing bugs "as you go" provides damage control because the earlier you learn of your mistakes, the less likely you are to repeat those mistakes.

◆ Bugs are a form of negative feedback that keep fast but sloppy programmers in check. If you don't allow programmers to work on new features until they have fixed all their bugs, you prevent sloppy programmers from spreading half-implemented features throughout the product—they're too busy fixing bugs. If you allow programmers to ignore their bugs, you lose that regulation.

◆ By keeping the bug count near zero, you have a much easier time predicting when you'll finish the product. Instead of trying to guess how long it will take to finish 32 features and 1742 bug-fixes, you just have to guess how long it will take to finish the 32 features. Even better, you're often in a position to drop the unfinished features and ship what you have.

As I said in *Writing Solid Code,* I believe these observations apply to any software development project, and I'll repeat the advice I ended with there:

> If you are not already fixing bugs as you find them, let Microsoft's negative experience be a lesson to you. You can learn through your own hard experience, or you can learn from the costly mistakes of others.

———◆———

Don't fix bugs later; fix them now.

———◆———

When programmers fix their bugs matters a great deal, just as when servers make new coffee matters a great deal. Requiring programmers to fix their bugs the moment they're found introduces a small system into

---

"Unacceptably Slow"

Some groups at Microsoft have broadened the traditional concept of what constitutes a bug to include any flaw that has to be addressed before the product is shipped. In these groups, a feature could be considered buggy simply because it was unacceptably slow. The feature might function without error, but the fact that it would still require work before it was ready to ship would be considered a bug.

If they have a policy of fixing bugs as they're found, groups that define bugs so broadly are forced early on to define what is and is not "unacceptably slow." In fact, they're forced to define all their quality bars early on. The result: programmers don't waste time rewriting unshippable code, at least not more than once or twice, before they learn what quality levels they're aiming for.

The drawback to this approach is that some programmers might waste time writing complex, efficient code, say, when straightforward code would do just fine. But such a tendency could be easily detected (and corrected) in regular code reviews.

---

the development process that protects the product in many ways. In addition to the benefits I described in *Writing Solid Code,* the system produces these good side effects:

◆   The constant message to programmers is that bugs are serious and must not be ignored. This point is emphasized right from the start of the project and receives perpetual reinforcement.

◆   Programmers become solely responsible for fixing their own bugs. No longer do the careful programmers have to help fix the bugs of the sloppy programmers. Instead, the careful programmers get to implement the features the sloppy programmers can't get to because they're stuck fixing bugs in their earlier features. The effect is that programmers are rewarded for being careful. Justice!

◆   If programmers are fixing bugs as they're found, the project can't possibly have a runaway bug-list. In fact, the bug-list can never sneak up and threaten your project's timely delivery. How could it? You're always fighting the monster while it's little.

◆   Finally, and perhaps most important, requiring programmers to fix their bugs as they find them makes it quite apparent if a particular programmer needs more training—his or her schedule starts slipping, alerting you to a problem that might otherwise go unnoticed.

Whether you realize it or not, your development process is filled with little systems that affect the quality of the product and the course of the project. That coffee shop manager with the mark on his pot understood the power of developing a system and used that power to his advantage. You can do the same with your projects, coming up with little systems that naturally give you the results you want.

———◆———

Actively use systems that improve
the development process.

———◆———

The E-Mail Trap

Electronic mail is a wonderful tool. I can't imagine working efficiently without it. Having said that, I have to add that when it isn't handled wisely, e-mail can destroy your productivity.

I've found that newly hired programmers allow e-mail to constantly interrupt their work. I don't mean that they're sending too much e-mail; I mean that they're stopping to read every new message as it arrives. New employees don't get much mail that they have to respond to; most e-mail they receive consists of passive information that's just making the rounds. You know, things like the closing price of Microsoft stock, what Spencer Katt had to say about this or that company that week, the business news wire releases for the day, and so on. This stuff trickles in throughout the day.

New employees tend to leave their e-mail readers running and to stop every 5 minutes to check out the latest "blip." They never get any work done because their entire day is broken into 5-minute time slices.

To combat this tendency, I routinely tell new hires to respond to their e-mail in batches: "Read it when you arrive in the morning, when you return from lunch, and just before you leave for the day." That tiny system for e-mail reading—governing only *when* they read their mail—allows developers to get their work done because the work is no longer subject to constant interruption.

The developers are reading the same number of messages; that hasn't changed. They're just reading those messages more efficiently and doing their other work more efficiently as a consequence.

LEANING ON CRUTCHES?

I've described using such trivial systems to programmers and leads on many occasions, and every once in a while I'll run into somebody who thinks systems are a bad idea. Such a person usually maintains that systems are a crutch: "You're cheating those people out of a learning experience. The next job they go to, they'll not have learned anything."

As much as I believe in using systems, I do take seriously the concern these people express. As you'll see throughout the book, I believe you must continually work to improve the skills of each member of your team. I just don't believe that the project has to be a casualty of that learning experience.

The beauty of setting up a system is that team members don't have to immediately grasp the rationales behind the system in order for it to work. But don't keep the rationales behind your system a secret. I'd urge you to do just the opposite: fully describe the thinking behind the system you set up and what you expect the system to accomplish. In time, the team members will begin to appreciate the thinking behind the system and probably start to add improvements that will make it even more effective. Encourage your team to understand and improve the systems you put in place.

---◆---

Don't use systems in lieu of training.
Use systems and explain why you
expect them to work.

---◆---

Please Pass the Popcorn

Well-designed systems for working are valuable because they can nudge people into doing what's best for the product. A strategy is valuable because it condenses a body of experience into a simple attack plan that anybody can immediately understand and act on. A collection of such strategies can catapult an individual (or a team) to a higher level of productivity, quality, or whatever it is that the strategies focus on.

As a lead, you should encourage your team to share the strategies they've found to be effective in achieving project goals and priorities. My highest priority for software products is that they always be bug-free, for instance, but as we all know, achieving that state is much easier to talk about than to accomplish. Even so, I can look at different programmers and see that some have much lower bug rates than others. Why? The programmers with lower bug rates have a better understanding of how to prevent bugs and of how to effectively find any bugs that do creep into their code. They have better strategies for writing bug-free programs.

To encourage developers to come up with strategies that result in bug-free code, I have them ask themselves two questions each time they track down the cause of a bug:

How could I have prevented this bug?

and

How could I have easily (and automatically) detected this bug?

As you can probably imagine, any programmer who habitually asks these questions begins to spot error-prone coding habits and starts to weed them out of his or her coding practice. Such a programmer also begins to discover better strategies for finding bugs. Of course, most programmers would, in time, develop such strategies anyway, but by constantly asking those two questions, they more rapidly—and consciously—learn how to prevent and detect bugs. As with anything else, if you systematically focus on an area, you get better results than you would if you haphazardly wandered over to it every now and then. There's no magic here.

As a lead, you can ask yourself similar questions for each problem you encounter:

How can I avoid this problem in the future?

and

What can I learn from this mistake/experience?

These are critical questions that successful leads habitually ask themselves as they actively improve their skills. Some leads forever repeat the same mistakes because they fail to ask these questions and act on their findings.

Of course, the quality of the questions you ask will determine the quality of the strategies you derive from them. Consider these two questions:

Why do our schedules always slip?

vs.

How can we prevent schedule slipping in the future?

Although the questions are quite similar, would you give the same answers to both? I doubt it. I doubt it because the first question gets you to focus on all the reasons your schedules slip: you have too many dependencies on other teams, your tools are lousy, your boss is a bozo and always gets in your way, and so on. The second question gets you to focus on what you can do to prevent slipping in the future: reducing your dependency on other groups, buying better tools, establishing a new work arrangement with your boss. The questions focus on different aspects of the problem—one on causes, the other on prevention—so the quality of the answers for the two is different. The first question elicits complaints; the second question elicits an *attack plan.*

Even if the questions you ask yourself have the right focus, they may not be precise enough to elicit effective strategies. Just as goals gain power as you increase their detail, questions become more powerful as you increase their precision. Let's take a look at another question:

How can we consistently hit our ship dates?

Some leads who asked that question might decide to pressure their teams to work overtime by threatening them. Others might decide to bribe their teams to work overtime with bonuses or free dinners or by projecting blockbuster movies at midnight and passing out buckets of popcorn. (Don't laugh. It has happened.)

But suppose those leads had asked a more precise, and in my opinion more beneficial, question:

How can we consistently hit our ship dates, without having developers work overtime?

The leads would obviously get a different kind of answer because threats or midnight movies wouldn't answer the requirements posed by this more precise question. The leads would have to toss out any "solution" that called for getting their teams to work overtime. They'd be forced to search for other possibilities. They might decide that to hit their ship dates without demanding overtime work they'd have to hire more developers. That's a possibility, but not one that companies usually like to consider, at least not until all other approaches have been exhausted. To eliminate that unacceptable solution from consideration, I'll increase the precision of the question even further:

> *How can we consistently hit our ship dates, without having*
> *developers work overtime, and without hiring additional people?*

The question now eliminates two undesirable solutions, forcing leads to think more creatively and, not incidentally, to focus more on the work itself. Maybe a lead would decide that it wasn't so critical, after all, that his team write all the code in the product: he could hire a short-term consultant, or the team could use a code library another team might have offered them just the month before, or they could even buy a fully documented commercial library, which could cut their development time dramatically. Maybe they'd decide to cut features that, upon reflection, they'd see wouldn't really add much value to the product.

The Ideal Question

As we'll see throughout this book, there are numerous ways to increase productivity without resorting to 80-hour weeks. When you ask questions to elicit solutions, keep in mind that question from Chapter 1: What am I *ultimately* trying to accomplish? No lead is ultimately trying to get people to work overtime; most are in fact ultimately trying to get more work done in a shorter period of time.

The simplest technique for zeroing in on the best question to ask is to envision how you would ideally like your project to run and to tailor your question so that it reflects that ideal. Wouldn't your ideal project be one in which you made perfect estimates, you hit every feature milestone, nobody worked overtime, and all concerned thoroughly enjoyed their work? That's a lot to ask, but if you tailor your questions to reflect that ideal, you'll come up with the solutions that will bring you closer to those goals.

The point is that by asking a more precise question, one that takes into account the results they'd ideally like to see, leads force themselves to weed out all the less than ideal solutions—the ones they might have glommed onto simply because they were the first solutions that presented themselves. Asking increasingly detailed questions stimulates the thinking process that leads to inventive solutions.

Ask detailed questions that yield
strategies and systems that help to
achieve your ideal project goals.

GOTOS HAVE THEIR PLACE

As you go about creating and promoting strategies, regularly remind the development team that the strategies are not rules that are meant to be followed 100 percent of the time. You want to be sure that people are thinking about what they're doing, not blindly following a set of rules even when those rules don't make sense.

One coding strategy that many programmers treat as an ironclad rule is "Don't use goto statements." But experienced programmers generally agree that there are a few special scenarios—mostly dealing with complex error-handling—in which using goto statements actually improves the clarity of code. When I see that a programmer has implemented that kind of error-handling code, scrupulously avoiding gotos, I usually raise the issue with the programmer.

"Did you consider using gotos to improve this code?" I ask.

"What? Of course not! Gotos are evil and create totally unreadable spaghetti code. Only incompetent programmers use gotos."

"Well, there are a few cases in which using gotos can make sense," I tell the programmer. "This is one of those cases. Let's compare your code to an implementation that uses a goto statement." I hand the programmer the goto version. "Which implementation is easier to read and understand?"

"The goto version," the programmer will usually reluctantly admit.

"So which implementation will you use in the future?"

"Mine, because it doesn't use any gotos."

"Wait, I thought you just agreed that the goto version was easier to read and understand."

"It is easier to read and understand, but using gotos can cause the compiler to generate less than optimal code."

"Let's assume that you're right, that the compiler generates some less than optimal code in this function. How often would this coding scenario show up?"

"Not very often, I guess."

"And which is a higher coding priority for the project, code clarity or a questionable efficiency gain?"

"Code clarity."

"So which version is easier to read and understand *and* follows our project priorities?"

At this point there is usually a long pause.

"But gotos are *bad*," the programmer blurts out in a last, pitiful protest.

I'll be the first to admit that there aren't many places in which using gotos actually clarifies the code; you can be sure that whenever I'm reviewing code and I see a goto, alarms start going off. I am not pro-goto—the presence of a goto usually does indicate a quick and dirty

---

Show Me Code!

Perhaps the most thorough discussion ever published about the pros and cons of using gotos can be found in Chapter 16 of Steve McConnell's *Code Complete*. In addition to showing those instances in which the judicious use of a goto can actually improve code, McConnell fully delineates the arguments against and for gotos and goes on to show how often the goto debate is phony. He finishes up with a list of articles that have exhaustively covered the use of gotos, including Edsger Dijkstra's original letter to the editor on the subject and Donald Knuth's example-rich "Structured Programming with go to Statements." As McConnell points out, "[the goto debate] erupts from time to time in most workplaces, textbooks, and magazines, but you won't hear anything that wasn't fully explored 20 years ago."

design hacked together while the programmer sat in front of the key-board with a sugar buzz. But while I'm generally against using gotos, I'm even more against blindly following rules when they don't make sense and actually work to the detriment of the product.

That's the major drawback to strategies. If you push them as invio-lable rules, you risk having team members do stupid things.

I know instructors mean well when they advise programmers not to use gotos, but I wish they would explain that gotos should be used rarely, instead of never. Even better, I wish that they'd demonstrate those few cases in which using gotos actually makes sense—it's not as if there are dozens of scenarios they'd have to cover. The problem, I think, is that many instructors were taught that gotos should never be used and they pass this advice on with ever-growing fervor. The mere pres-ence of a goto is enough for some instructors (and programmers) to de-clare the code terrible, just as any form of nudity is enough for some people to proclaim a film immoral.

There are very few programming strategies that should be en-forced as rules, and you need to make that clear. Otherwise, you may end up with developers blindly following a rule in situations in which it doesn't make sense. This disclaimer certainly applies to all the strategies in this book.

*Don't present strategies as ironclad
rules; present strategies as guidelines
to be followed most of the time.*

FEEDBACK LOOPS

Electrical engineers use the concept of positive and negative feedback loops to describe the characteristics of a particular type of circuit, one in which the output of the circuit is fed back as an input to that same cir-cuit. Here's a picture.

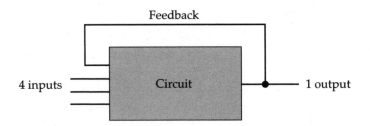

With the output contributing to its own result, such circuits behave in one of two ways: the output amplifies itself, so that the stronger it is, the stronger it gets; or just the opposite occurs, so that the stronger the output is, the weaker it gets. Feedback loops in which the output amplifies itself are known as positive feedback loops, and those in which the output weakens itself are known as negative feedback loops. From this admittedly simplified description of the two types of loops, it might seem that positive feedback loops are great because they leverage their own power whereas negative feedback loops are worthless because every time the output gets stronger, the effect is counteracted. In fact, negative feedback loops are far more useful than positive loops.

If you've ever been in an auditorium and heard a speaker and a microphone together cause an ear-shattering screech that could wake Elvis, you've been the victim of a positive feedback loop. The microphone has picked up and reamplified its own output, driving the amplifier into overload. That's the common problem with positive feedback loops: they typically overload themselves.

A negative feedback loop would take a high output and use it to reduce the loop's future output. Imagine welding the brake pedal of your car to the accelerator: step on the gas a bit, and the brakes go on a bit to counteract the acceleration; floor the gas, and you floor the brakes too. The stronger the output, the harder the circuit counteracts it. Such behavior may sound as useless as going into overload all the time, but negative feedback loops don't need to completely dominate the output; they just need to exert enough force to regulate and stabilize the circuit.

I've been talking about electrical circuits, but you'll find feedback loops in all sorts of systems, whether systems for personal relationships or for software development. Some of the feedback loops develop without conscious intention, and others are designed, but whatever their origins, you can achieve greater control over your project by becoming aware of feedback loops and making deliberate use of them.

Bugs, for example, are a common "output" of writing code. Wouldn't it be wonderful if you could design a negative feedback loop into your development process so that whenever the bug count grew, something would counteract that growth with equal force? We've already talked about exactly such a feedback loop:

> *Require that programmers fix their bugs the moment they're found.*

If a programmer's code never has bugs, the requirement that bugs be fixed the moment they're found will never affect her and she can happily implement new features. But if a programmer writes code that's riddled with bugs, the requirement will kick in in full force, pulling that programmer off the implementation of new features and back to work on bugs, preventing her from spreading sloppy work throughout the program. The more bugs the programmer has, the harder the brakes are applied. The requirement that bugs be fixed immediately implements a negative feedback loop designed to keep the product bug-free at all times. And, of course, the practice gives you all those other benefits I mentioned earlier in the chapter—the relative ease with which recent bugs can be fixed, the speed with which programmers learn from fresh mistakes, easier prediction of project completion dates, and so on.

Negative feedback loops can hurt as well as help, though. Do you remember that lead I talked about in Chapter 1, the one who required his team members to submit status reports, attend status meetings, and then write follow-up reports on any insights they had come up with during the meetings? That lead was trying to get as much good information from the team as he could. Unfortunately, he'd set up a negative feedback loop that thwarted a desirable output. He wanted to hear any ideas his team members might come up with to solve a problem, but by asking them to write up those thoughts in reports, he discouraged them from saying anything. His system made people clam up—the more you spoke, the longer the report you had to write. Nobody liked writing those reports, so they learned to keep quiet. Just the opposite of what the lead was hoping for. Backfire.

You must also be careful not to unwittingly set up destructive *positive* feedback loops. If you base raises and bonuses on the number of new lines of code programmers write—and rewriting bad code doesn't count—don't be surprised if the programmers, over time, develop the

---

Negative Feedback Is Not Negative Reinforcement

Don't confuse negative feedback with negative reinforcement. I think of negative reinforcement as scolding, berating, or threatening an employee—like whipping a horse to get it to do what you want. Or, if an employee steps out of line, WHACK, giving him or her a solid dose of negative reinforcement to discourage stepping out of line in the future.

That kind of management style is reprehensible and certainly *not what I'm advocating*. Think about the negative feedback requirement that programmers fix their bugs as they're found. A programmer shouldn't be anxious about having to fix his bugs as they're reported. The requirement might have put him in a position he doesn't like—being stuck on the same feature for days on end—but that's very different from filling him with a sense of dread. The goal is to have the right things happen easily and naturally, without personal distress—not to assert who is boss or to put the employee in his or her place.

Many years ago at Microsoft, there were a couple of leads who, when a project was not running smoothly, would round up the development team and proceed to tell them that they were the worst programmers at Microsoft, that they weren't worthy of calling themselves Microsoft programmers, and other such nonsense. I'm not sure what those leads were trying to accomplish, but if their goal was to get the teams to rally and try harder, they picked a pretty strange way of doing it. As I'm sure you can imagine, those leads only succeeded in angering and depressing their development teams. Furthermore, in every case of which I was aware, the problems with the project were management related—the projects had no clear focus or were simply too ambitious. The programmers on those projects weren't any better or worse than other programmers in the company, and berating them didn't change anything for the better—only for the worse.

---

habit of sticking with their clunky first-draft code and patching flawed designs with new code instead of doing badly needed rewrites. You might intend the bonus to be an incentive for programmers to be more productive, but the long-term result would probably be a company full of programmers who are satisfied with slapped-together implementations.

I hope you'll take two points away from this discussion. First, whenever you design a new system, try to include beneficial negative feedback loops that help to keep the project on track. Second, consider the long-term effects of any feedback loops you decide to employ; make sure there are no feedback loops that can ultimately cripple the effort.

———◆———

Deliberately use negative feedback loops in your systems to achieve desirable side effects.

Beware of feedback loops that create undesirable side effects.

———◆———

THE SIMPLER, THE BETTER

Finally, make sure that the systems and strategies you come up with are easy to understand and follow.

Consider some of the systems I've covered: writing in longhand, using two kinds of coffee cups, watching a line on a coffee pot, reading e-mail in batches, fixing bugs the moment you find them. These systems are trivial, not hulking processes that will bog down the whole operation.

One tendency at workplaces is for simple processes to blossom into time-consuming busy-work because people get caught up in creating processes instead of working on the product. Having programmers ask, "How could I have prevented this bug?" is simple. Taking that system a step further and asking every programmer to write a "prevention report" for every bug he or she encounters is altogether different. All of a sudden the systematic asking of a simple question has turned into a cumbersome process. Such process growth is as natural as the growth of brambles, and you must actively keep that growth cut back.

Remember, the overall goal is to stay focused on improving the product, not on fulfilling process requirements. You want to gain the benefits that systems can provide and jettison the drawbacks. Well-designed systems and appropriately applied strategies accomplish both of these goals.

HIGHLIGHTS

◆ Simple work systems can produce dramatic results. Take a good look at the processes your team members are already following. Are there problems with those processes? Are they too time-consuming? Too error-prone? Are they frustrating and counterproductive in some way? If they are, look for simple changes you can make to improve those processes.

◆ As you put systems in place, explain the purposes behind them so that the development team can understand what aspect of the product the systems are meant to improve. This openness will educate team members over time and also enable them to intelligently improve the systems and create new, better ones.

◆ Refine the questions you ask as you look for solutions to problems. Develop the ability to ask precise questions to increase the quality of your answers. Unfortunately, it's not enough to be precise. A precise but wrong question will get you a bad answer. Be sure the question you ask focuses on what you're ultimately trying to achieve, on your ideal solution. Don't ask, "How can we get programmers to work longer hours?" Ask, "How can programmers get more done in less time?"

◆ The more appealing or effective a strategy is, the more people on your team will want to treat it as an ironclad rule. Remind your team that even the best strategies don't apply to every situation. "Avoid using gotos" is a strategy that can lead programmers to write more readable code. But you should encourage programmers to see that they should set aside even this strategy when avoiding gotos would make the code less readable.

◆   Whenever you create a feedback loop, be sure to consider the side effects and the long-term effects. The best feedback loops enhance the desirable aspects over time while simultaneously reducing the negative effects.

3

OF STRATEGIC IMPORTANCE

I like to think that my projects are always on course, but in fact they never are. Sometimes a project is ahead of schedule, sometimes behind, but always close. The project zigzags along an imaginary line that plots the ideal course.

Even the best-run projects are never on course. But if you let a project coast, not knowing how far off course it is, you're going to wake up one morning to find that you've zigged so much that you can't zag enough to correct. In that respect, a project is like a rocket aimed at the moon—a tiny fraction of a degree off, and the rocket will miss the moon by thousands of miles. If your project is off track, even slightly, it will steadily get further off track unless you make regular, tiny adjustments to its course.

Effective leaders understand this principle. They take consistent, daily steps to nudge their projects back onto those imaginary trajectories. In this chapter, we'll look at simple, effective strategies you can use to keep your projects on track.

FREEWAY OVERPASSES

I'm convinced that the main reason projects go astray is that the people running the projects don't spend enough time thinking about how to keep them running smoothly. They don't anticipate problems and instead wait until problems show up. By then, it's too late. What could have taken 30 seconds of extra thought to prevent a month ago is now going to take hours or days to correct. This is known as "working in reaction," and many leads seem to do it.

The alternative to simply reacting is to actively look for potential problems and take little steps to avoid them. Suppose one of those house movers I talked about in Chapter 1 had hopped into his flatbed truck and started slowly on his way along the route to the house's new location, only to turn a corner and be blocked by a low freeway overpass. Oops—gotta retrace at least part of the route and have the same overhead power and phone lines taken down again. Or what if the planned route looked flat on the map but had hills too steep to pull a house up? Or what if the route were usually passable but road crews were out that week resurfacing a stretch of the road? Each of these obstacles could have been foreseen by the "house lead" if only he had taken the time to drive the route the day before and then again an hour before starting the house rolling. Can you conceive of a house lead's not taking that step? Why then do so many software leads fail to drive ahead and look for obstacles that could easily be avoided, allowing their projects to be stalled by those obstacles?

Leads don't always look ahead because that's harder to do than not looking ahead. How many times have you heard a lead faced with an unexpected obstacle say, "I could have prevented this if I'd spent time thinking about it earlier"? In my experience, few leads make such an admission. Rather, leads tend to be not at all surprised that something unexpected has come up. After all, they think, it happens to everybody, all the time. It's normal.

To get out of this mind set, you need to work proactively instead of re-actively. There are many techniques you can use to train yourself to work proactively, but they can all be boiled down to a fairly simple practice:

Regularly stop what you're doing and look ahead, making little adjustments now *to avoid big obstacles later on.*

Leads don't have trouble spotting the already big obstacles coming up—say, having to support Windows NT once the regular Windows version is done, or having to find time to create a demonstration-quality product in time for COMDEX. It's the little obstacles that blindside people, the ones that blossom into huge obstacles if they aren't foreseen and handled early, while they are still manageable. That kind of foresight is like stopping for gas before heading to the ski slopes—taking that simple step could prevent you from having to make a long, snowy trek because you ran out of gas halfway up the mountain.

The habit I've developed and used successfully for more than a decade is to spend the first 10 or 15 minutes of each day making a list of answers to this question:

What can I do today *that would help keep the project on track for the next few months?*

It's a simple question, but if you ask it regularly, it will give you all the information you'll need to protect your projects from being clobbered by problems you could have foreseen. Note that the tasks you'll list probably won't be complex. In fact, most such tasks are simple and can be completed in a few minutes. My own list of tasks is usually like this one:

◆ Order the MIPS and Alpha processor manuals so that they'll be here well before Hubie needs them.

◆ Send e-mail to the Word team reminding them that they must make additional feature requests by Monday if they'll need those features in our next library release.

◆ Send e-mail to the Graphics lead to verify that the Graphics library we're depending on is still on track for delivery three weeks from now.

None of these tasks would take me much time to do, but they could save me an enormous amount of time later on. Ordering that MIPS processor manual may not seem like a big deal, but if the manual takes three weeks to arrive, that could cause a three-week slip in the MIPS work. How long does it take to order a manual? About 10 minutes? You could spend 10 minutes *now* and have the manual in time, or spend 10 minutes *and* three weeks later on. . .

Often, by means of such little tasks, you can discover that the Graphics lead thinks he might slip two weeks, or that the Word group does have another request but didn't think there was any need to hurry up to tell you. Without checking (looking ahead), you could get caught off guard by a slip of the Graphics library schedule, or you could have a last minute fire when the Word team realizes that the feature they need hasn't made it into the next release of the library.

In an ideal world the Graphics lead would tell you well in advance that his project was going to slip, but how many times does that really happen? In my experience, almost never, because leads don't want to alarm anybody until it's clear that they are definitely going to slip— three days before the scheduled drop.

———◆———

Each day, ask, "What can I do today to help keep the project on track for the next few months?"

———◆———

BAD INTELLIGENCE

During the development of Word for Windows, I was asked to take a look at an internal code library written by non-Word programmers. The library was a dialog manager whose purpose was to isolate the operating system from Microsoft's applications, allowing programmers to create dialogs without worrying about whether the applications were going to run on Windows, the Macintosh, or some other system.

I was called in to find out why the library was so slow—the Word for Windows project lead and program manager were irritated by the delay between the time a dialog was invoked and the time it was fully displayed and ready for user interaction. The programmers working on the dialog manager had profiled their code and had made numerous optimizations, but the Word group was still dissatisfied and was making a ruckus, slowly ruining the library's reputation within the company. Other teams who were planning to use the library had begun to back off.

When I talked with Word's program manager to better understand the speed problem and find out what performance would be acceptable to the Word group, he handed me a list of acceptable display times— their quality bar. Each dialog had to be fully displayed in the time indicated next to its name. The program manager then demonstrated by bringing Word up and invoking a dialog with one hand while starting a stopwatch with the other. "See," he said, showing me the stopwatch. "This dialog takes too much time." Visually the dialog itself didn't seem to be that slow to me, so I reached over and invoked the dialog a second time to get another look. The dialog appeared almost instantly. I pointed out that the second invocation was well under the acceptable time limit.

"It's always fine the second time," he said. "We're only concerned about the first time, when the dialog is invoked after a period of inactivity. That's when the dialogs are too slow."

I understood the problem and went back to my office to look at the code. What I found was startling. It turned out that, at the time, Word itself contained an optimization that overrode the normal Windows code-swapping algorithm. The optimization was kicking out all "unnecessary" code segments after a certain period of inactivity, and that optimization was kicking out every byte of code related to the dialog manager. A little measuring showed that even if the dialog code were executed instantaneously, no dialog would pass its speed test; Word simply took too long to reload those "unnecessary" segments.

So the speed problem that the Word people had been complaining about wasn't a speed problem at all, but was instead a code-swapping problem. The Word team thought the dialog manager was much too slow, yet the dialog team couldn't see where the slowdown was—the code seemed fast enough in the library's test application, and there was no reason the dialog manager should have behaved differently when linked into Word. Of course, the test application didn't override the Windows swapping algorithm.

The Word team had been complaining about the speed problem for months, and the dialog team had been working long, hard hours to optimize code and algorithms in the library, hoping that each latest round of improvements would finally be enough to satisfy Word's requirements. Had anybody stopped to profile Word's handling of the dialog manager

---

The Debugging Game

Many programmers don't do research during debugging sessions. Some programmers try to fix a bug by jumping into the code, making a change, and then rerunning the program to see if the bug went away. When they see that the bug still exists, they make another change and do another run. Nope, that didn't work, better try something else. . .

I know that some programmers play the "maybe this is the problem" game because whenever they get a difficult bug for which none of their guesses seems to work, they ask me, their lead, what they should try next. The "next?" question is a dead-giveaway that they're playing the guessing game instead of actually looking for the cause of the bug.

In my experience, the most efficient way to track down a bug is to set a breakpoint in the debugger, determine which piece of data is bad, and then backtrack to the origin of that bad data, even if it means mucking around in data structures, following pointers, and other such tedious stuff. There's no question that it's sometimes easier to guess where a bug is and then fix it with a lucky hit, but it's consistently more efficient to look at the actual data and backtrack to its corruption.

I'm also skeptical of programmers who find bugs by "looking at the code." Andrew Koenig's *C Traps and Pitfalls* is an entire book of C examples that look perfectly correct but in fact contain subtle bugs. And Gimpel Software's marketing campaign for their PC-Lint product features magazine ads each month that point out obviously correct, yet buggy, code.

Looking for bugs by looking at the source code is lazy and inefficient; it shouldn't take a programmer any more time to view the code in a debugger, watching the *data* as he or she progressively steps through each line of source.

code, he or she would have seen that no amount of code optimization could have solved the problem the Word team was complaining about.

Granted, it's not always reasonable for a library team to regularly build and test all of the dozens (or sometimes thousands) of applications they support. It does make sense for a library team to use an aggressive—and I stress *aggressive* here—test application specifically designed to exercise every aspect of the library. But in this case, the Word team had been complaining loudly for quite some time, and the library team had found no obvious problems in their test application's use of the library. Somebody well before me should have built and profiled Word to see why it was behaving so differently from the test application. A little bit of research early on could have saved months of misguided optimization work, and the library probably wouldn't have developed an undeserved reputation.

As a lead, you should keep a wary eye open for any problem that persists and make sure that you, or someone, stops to do some focused research to figure out what's going wrong. The research may be tedious and time-consuming, but that's better than spending weeks or months trying to fix the wrong problem.

Don't waste time working on the wrong problem. Always determine what the real problem is before you try to make a fix.

OUTRAGEOUS MENUS

One time, the technical lead for the Windows-like user interface library I talked about in Chapter 1 came to me in a panic. He had just received a request from an application group for a feature that would take weeks to implement, yet our delivery schedules were pretty much carved in stone—we were not in a position to slip, at least not without severe repercussions. I asked him what the application group's request was.

"They want a modified form of our drop-down list boxes. They want to be able to use the list boxes outside dialogs; they want to be able to display the list boxes without their scroll bars and to be able to dim some of the list box items. They also want to be able to click on a list box item and have it automatically pop up another list box, but if you move the mouse back into the original list box, the new list box automatically disappears." Whew!

I had to agree: implementing those requests would kill our delivery schedules. After hearing a full description of the request, though, I wasn't concerned—anything that unusual didn't belong in a shared library. My initial thought was to give the application group the code for the standard list boxes so that they could implement those quirky list boxes themselves. Still, I was puzzled by their request. What were they going to use those list boxes for? I assumed it must be for some new-fangled user interface I'd yet to see. So before saying we wouldn't do it, I asked the technical lead to find out what the application group was going to do with those bizarre list boxes. He returned a while later, a wide grin on his face.

"They want to use the list boxes to simulate hierarchical menus, like the menus in Windows and on the Macintosh."

Now I knew why the technical lead was grinning: we already had an add-on library that fully supported hierarchical menus; the other group was simply unaware of the fact.

I bring this story up because it's common for groups to ask for something without explaining the reason behind their request. I see this all the time, even outside work. At a diner I sometimes go to for an early lunch, people occasionally come in and, seeing that everybody is still eating breakfast, ask the waitress, "How late are you going to be serving breakfast?" I've seen dozens of hungry people turn on their heels, mumbling, "I really want lunch," and walk out the door before the waitress can tell them they can order lunch. The lunch menu is available around the clock.

Why did those people ask about breakfast when what they really wanted to know was "Can I get lunch?" Their thinking went off on a tangent that seemed to be related to what they wanted, and they asked the wrong question. It happens all the time. I'm sensitive to the problem of asking the wrong question, but I still find myself asking my wife, Beth, when she'll be home from her evening soccer game—when what I really want to know is what time she'd like to have dinner.

Asking the wrong question or raising the wrong issue seems to be a common problem, and if you're aware of this tendency in people, you can save everybody time and effort by making it a habit to determine what the other people are actually trying to accomplish. If what they're trying to achieve isn't clear from their request, be sure to ask them what they're trying to do before you spend much time working on the request—or you refuse it.

———◆———

People often ask for something other than what they really need. Always determine what they are trying to accomplish before dealing with any request.

———◆———

First Define the Context

A good way to avoid miscommunication in your own requests is to first define the context of what you're trying to accomplish and then make your specific request. Suppose the programmer from the application group who made the list box request had started his e-mail this way:

```
We need hierarchical menus for the next release of our
product. Since drop-down list boxes are similar to menus,
we think we can simulate hierarchical menus if you can
provide us with a modified form of drop-down list boxes
that allows us to. . .
```

If we had received that e-mail message, our technical lead wouldn't have panicked, he wouldn't have had to meet with me to figure out how to handle the request, and he could have immediately told the other group about the add-on library's support for hierarchical menus. Even more important, I wouldn't have almost rejected their request—in which case they could have spent weeks reimplementing a library we already had.

By first telling people what you're trying to accomplish, you get them focused on helping with your ultimate need, not on one possible solution to that need.

JUST SAY NO

Suppose we hadn't bothered to find out why that group needed those weird list boxes and had simply turned down their request. Do you think they would have said, "OK, we understand. Thanks anyway"? Maybe. But plenty of groups would have argued that as custodians of the user interface library we had a responsibility to maintain the code and provide new features when they were asked for—that giving them some source code to adapt just wouldn't do.

Of course, the easiest way to resolve such disagreements is to knuckle under and agree to do the work, and that's exactly what I've seen many leads in troubled groups do. These leads would rather defuse a tense situation than fight for what's best for the product or their team.

Sometimes a group will make a perfectly reasonable request that, because your schedule is full, you can't meet, and you're put in the position of saying No to that group. I know from experience that there are plenty of leads who, to avoid the confrontation, will agree to fulfill the request anyway, without having any idea how they'll get the work done on time. Somehow, they think, they'll pull it off. And, of course, they rarely do.

What these leads don't realize is that by agreeing to work they shouldn't do or can't do they are dodging a bit of short-term pain in exchange for a lot of long-term pain—and not just for themselves, but for every single member of their teams. Which do you suppose is more painful all the way around: showing the lead of a dependent group why you can't possibly fulfill a request given your current schedule, or promising to finish the work on a specific date and then missing that date by six weeks?

Consider the difference. When the lead of the dependent group makes a request, the date on which that request needs to be fulfilled is often in the distant future; if you can't fulfill the request, there's plenty of time for you and the lead of the dependent group to consider alternatives. The only way you can be considered the villain is to reject the request without even trying to help the other lead work something out. Compare that approach to caving in and agreeing to deliver some new functionality, thinking you will somehow get the work done—and missing the deadline you agreed to. Not only did your group miss its deadline, but you've possibly caused all the groups depending on you to miss their deadlines as well.

Think of it this way: if you were buying a house and needed a loan, which bank would upset you more, the one whose loan officer turned you down immediately, or the one whose loan officer agreed to give you the loan but changed his mind two months later as you were signing the closing papers?

I'm not saying that you should turn down requests just so that you'll have a cushy schedule. I'm saying that you should never commit to a date you know you can't meet. It might be tempting to think that you'll somehow make the date, but that's usually just wishful thinking. There are enough slips in dates leads "know" they can make, let alone in the dates they're unsure of.

It's not easy to fight these little battles up front, but it beats having the company CEO sitting on your desk several weeks or months later demanding to know why you waited until Marketing's ads had hit the magazine stands before you confessed that you couldn't possibly make the dates you promised.

Don't Halt the Machinery

Fighting your battles up front puts a critical process in motion—the search for a true solution. If you were truthful and realistic about what your team could actually accomplish and said No when you knew you couldn't meet a date, *the search for a workable solution would continue.* Maybe the other group would do the work themselves, or maybe they'd split the work with you, or maybe they'd ask other groups in your organization if they had a similar piece of code already written, perhaps buried in the guts of some application. Who knows?

Saying No may be unpleasant, but it keeps the problem-solving machinery chugging away until somebody, somehow, can say Yes and believe in what he or she is saying.

Never commit to dates you know you can't meet. You'll hurt everybody involved.

I Failed to Say No

One time, the Word for MS-DOS team asked our user interface library team to implement a costly add-on feature in time for Word's upcoming beta release. We were booked solid with work, and I couldn't see any way to meet their date without slipping our own date and affecting the more than 20 other groups using the library. I explained to the Word group that we could—and would—do the work, just not in time for their deadline. I proposed that, if they definitely needed the feature that quickly, they implement the add-on themselves, turning it over to us when it was completed. We would document the feature for other teams, enhance our test application to cover the feature, and support and continue to enhance the feature in the future. The Word team was upset. They felt we should do the work since it was a feature that every other group would eventually want to use. They were right on that point, but that didn't change the fact that we couldn't implement the code in time for their release. We battled over this feature for nearly two months. I finally got so frustrated with the arguing that I broke down and agreed to do the feature, figuring that I'd temporarily pull a programmer off one of the other projects I was leading.

Well, I couldn't find that spare programmer, and the result was disastrous. We missed Word's deadline by weeks, and they screamed bloody murder. We missed all of our other commitments too—which we had been on track for—affecting those 20-odd other teams. More screaming. What a mess. If I had stuck to my guns and said No as I knew I should have, everybody would have been a whole lot better off, including the Word group.

THE NEED TO PLEASE

As a lead, you're going to be faced with all sorts of demands. To be effective, you must learn to say No when it's appropriate. Others may not like it, and they may think you're wrong, but you have to realize that you can't always please everybody—there are often just too many conflicting requests.

If you're in charge of a shared library, one team may ask you to add a feature that benefits only their project. If you say No, they'll probably get upset. If you say Yes to their unique request, another team may complain about the increase in the size of the library. These no-win situations come up all the time, particularly when you're responsible for code shared by multiple projects.

Which course of action should you take when you're faced with conflicting demands? That's where your detailed project goals come in handy. If one of your goals is to provide functionality that will be useful to all of the groups using your library, you know to reject a request that doesn't match that criterion. Sure, you'll get complaints, but it doesn't take much time to explain your reasons and to point out that if you implement one unusual request you'll have to implement the special requests made by every other project you're supporting, which will pull you off features *all* groups want and bloat the library with features that most groups don't need.

There seems to be a human need to please everybody, and that need can get leads into trouble because, in their desire to please everybody, they can do things that don't make sense for the project.

In my experience, people don't like having their requests rejected, but if you have solid reasons, they do understand and often appreciate your not giving them false promises.

———◆———

*Don't let wanting to please everybody
jeopardize your project. Use your goals
to guide your decisions.*

———◆———

> ### Not a Librarian?
>
> I've been assuming for the sake of argument that you're leading a library project, and I know that that's probably not the case. The points I'm making apply to most projects, though. Instead of having other leads making demands on your group, you might have a marketing team making the demands, or the folks who'll use the finished product. Every project will have some outside demands made upon it—even top secret projects always seem to have people outside the development team poking their noses in and making suggestions.

SUPERIOR SUGGESTIONS

You should be especially conscious of not trying to please everybody when it's your boss who makes suggestions. I'm not talking about resisting authority. I just want to point out that superiors can make bad suggestions just as everybody else can, particularly if they aren't aware of your goals, your priorities, and the technical challenges you face. If you want to be an effective lead, you must weigh all suggestions (or demands), no matter where they originate, against the needs of your project.

If your boss asks you to do something you think is a bad idea, explain your concerns before you undertake the work. Sometimes your boss will agree with your concerns and drop the suggestion; other times, your boss will acknowledge your concerns and go on to ask you to honor his or her suggestion anyway—in the best case scenario, providing solid justification. Regardless of the outcome, one or both of you will probably learn something.

I once reviewed a large piece of code written by an experienced programmer. I was surprised to find several critical design flaws in the code, flaws I wouldn't have expected to appear in code from this particular programmer. I asked the programmer why he had chosen such a design.

"I just did the implementation. Kirby did the design." Kirby was his lead at the time.

"How do you feel about this design?" I was curious.

"It's not the way I would have done it."

"Did you feel that way at the time you did the implementation?"

"Yeah," he shrugged. "But I had just started at Microsoft, Kirby was the lead, and I figured he was more experienced than I was. I thought he saw something in the design that I didn't. I didn't want to rock the boat."

In fact, Kirby was less experienced than the programmer who did the implementation. Kirby had simply been fortunate in getting a more experienced programmer on his team.

In another case in point, I was leading the teams responsible for Microsoft's 680x0 cross development system. Periodically Mort, a manager who had the power to change my development plans, would drop by my office to chat about the progress of the 680x0 C/C++ compiler. During every visit, Mort would get around to asking what grew to be the inevitable question, "How's the FORTRAN work going?"

Now, Mort knew darn well we weren't trying to produce a FORTRAN compiler, but he had a fondness for FORTRAN and felt there was a market for a good Macintosh FORTRAN compiler. Besides, creating a FORTRAN compiler out of the C/C++ work we were doing wasn't a bad idea—especially if you knew, as Mort did, that Microsoft's compilers use the common three-stage process described in most compiler texts:

Front end: Parse the specific language (C/C++, FORTRAN, Pascal, and so on) into a common intermediate language.

Optimizer: Perform all compiler optimizations (code motion, common subexpression elimination, strength reduction, and so on) on the intermediate language.

Back end: Generate optimized object code from the now-optimized intermediate language.

It's a bit more complicated than that, but you can see from this staging that to get a Macintosh compiler we needed only to write a new back end, one that generated Motorola 680x0 code instead of Intel 80x86 code.

In theory, then, once we had finished the 680x0 back end, we should have had our C/C++ compiler, plus FORTRAN and Pascal compilers—we just needed to link in the proper front ends. That's in theory. And that's why Mort was so interested in the possibility of a FORTRAN product. In reality, though, to build the FORTRAN compiler, we would have needed to fully implement the back end, and we were implementing only the 95 percent or so required by the C/C++ compiler.

Whenever Mort asked about the FORTRAN compiler, my answer was always the same: "We haven't done anything with that compiler." I would always follow with "But we're not doing anything in the back end that would prevent us from doing the FORTRAN work *at a later date.*"

Mort may have been right that there was a market for a good FORTRAN compiler on the Macintosh, but he was ignoring my team's project priorities. Just because there was a market and it was possible to create the product was no reason to temporarily halt work on the C/C++ compiler, which even he agreed had a significantly larger market potential. We wouldn't have had this discussion more than once if Mort hadn't been personally interested in the FORTRAN compiler. His personal interest was getting in the way of his business sense.

You must protect your project from outside manipulation, especially if the request comes from somebody who has clout. Somebody like Mort might not be right, but you might feel obliged to comply. In my early years as a lead, I probably would have bowed to Mort's pressure—I certainly caved in on similar requests. I eventually learned, though, that no matter where a request originates, you must question it. Does it improve the product? Is it strategically necessary according to your goals? Does it draw focus away from more important work? Will it be unnecessarily expensive or risky to implement? You must feel good about the answers to these questions, or you shouldn't do the work.

———◆———

You are responsible for your project.
Don't let ill-considered suggestions from
superiors disrupt your progress.

———◆———

THE TRUE COST

Why did Mort think that a Macintosh FORTRAN compiler was worth considering as a goal for the cross compiler project? Was it because people wouldn't stop calling Microsoft to ask why we didn't have such a compiler in our product line? Was it because coding in FORTRAN just made sense for the Macintosh environment? Of course not. The only reason the FORTRAN compiler was ever an issue was because one person who was fond of FORTRAN saw the possibility of getting a free FORTRAN compiler out of the C/C++ compiler work we were already doing.

I get excited about free products and features as much as the next person. There's that warm feeling you get when you realize that because you were such a brilliant designer, some unexpected functionality pops out. But free products are almost never strategic for your company, and free features are almost never strategic for your product. After all, if they were strategic, they would have been planned for, not serendipitously discovered.

It's interesting to note that we could also have gotten a Pascal compiler out of the C/C++ work by updating the older Pascal front end, but that idea never came up, even though the Macintosh was for many years a Pascal-only system—all the manuals and code examples from Apple Computer were in Pascal, and there were no serious development systems to compete with Apple's Pascal system. That's all changed now, of course; C/C++ has become the language of choice for the Macintosh. But if Microsoft were to ship a Macintosh compiler other than the C/C++ compiler, it would make far more sense, I think, to ship a Pascal, not a FORTRAN, compiler.

Mort was excited about the FORTRAN compiler because it was free, not because it was strategic. But how free would that FORTRAN compiler actually have been? To bring that free compiler to market, we would have had to

- Finish the remaining 5 percent or so of the back end to the compiler—a few programmer-months' worth of work.

- Find some way to enable FORTRAN programmers to interact in the Pascal-defined Macintosh operating system, which makes heavy use of Pascal records—something FORTRAN doesn't directly support. We would also have had to find some way to allow everything from Macintosh "traps" to Pascal-style strings in FORTRAN.

◆ Write manuals and help files to accompany the product.

◆ Fully test the compiler, linker, debugger, and other tools that would go in the box.

I'm sure I could think of additional tasks that would be necessary (say, training a product support team), but these are the obvious chores that come to mind. How free does that compiler sound now? Granted, the technical writers could probably pull the manuals and help files together fairly quickly if they used the existing 80x86 FORTRAN documents as a starting point. But there's no shortcut to testing a compiler. The Macintosh FORTRAN compiler would have required the same full-blown testing effort that any release of the 80x86 compiler would undergo.

That FORTRAN compiler was anything but free. Yes, the compiler was cheap compared to what it would cost starting from scratch. But "cheap" can still be expensive—just ask anybody who's bought a used Boeing 747 lately.

Free products and features—like free puppies—simply do not exist. Anytime you hear, or even think, the word "free," your immediate reaction should be resistance, not acceptance. Think of free products and features as you would those cold-call offers in which you're told that you'll get a free dream vacation in Bermuda for simply dropping by a showroom to hear about some new downtown luxury condominiums. In rare instances, such opportunities may be gold bars to be picked up, but in most cases, they're merely lead weights. If you want to keep your projects focused and under control, stick to the strategic work and leave those lead weights alone.

———◆———

There is no such thing as a free
product or feature.

———◆———

THE *LAYOFF* MACRO

Sometimes it's not a superior who makes questionable requests, but the marketing team. The scent of a big sale can cause the marketing team to consider features they'd never ask for in less heady situations. You need to protect your product from such requests.

When I was working on Microsoft Excel, the marketing team asked the development team to extend the product's macro language to include a new *LAYOFF* macro, which, as you can probably guess, was supposed to take a list of names and randomly pick people to lay off. A large corporate client had requested this *LAYOFF* macro so that they could lay people off without anybody being able to claim that the selections were biased. The company would be in a position to simply point to Excel to prove their innocence.

If you know Excel, you know that it doesn't contain such a *LAYOFF* macro. The task fell to me, and I refused to implement the request: I felt the macro would harm the product. My lead agreed, and for months we beat off the marketing team's persistent requests for the feature. Marketing felt they needed the macro to close the sale.

The feature became a big joke in the development group. "Let's do it, and we'll hardwire our names into the code so that we'll never be laid off! No, better than that, let's hardwire the marketers' names into the code so that they'll always be laid off!" Of course, none of that ever happened. In the end, Marketing wrote a simple user-defined macro to accomplish the same purpose. With that macro, the corporate client's request was met without Microsoft's having to build such an odious feature into the product.

In my experience, such ridiculous requests are rare. The marketing folks don't want to hurt the product. Just the opposite—they want the best product possible. But sometimes they're not too clear about what "best" means and ask for features you probably shouldn't implement. There are at least two types of such features: those that fill out feature sets and those that satisfy one of those product checklists you find in magazine reviews. Sometimes filling out feature sets or satisfying product checklists does improve the product, but just as often adding such features merely causes bloat and wastes development time.

The reason I say that—besides years of observation—is the motivation behind the requests. Think about it. Suppose the marketing team comes to you and says, "The Hewlett-Packard HP12c business calculator has these five functions that we don't yet support in our spreadsheet. We'd like you to add them to the standard set of functions." Would fulfilling such a request make for a strategic improvement to the product, or is it more likely that the request came about because a marketer realized, "Hey, we don't support the full set of HP12c features; we'd better add what we don't have"? Those additional features may actually be important, but if they are, why weren't they included in an earlier release? It's possible that those features simply weren't worth the time and effort. They still may not be.

Strategic Marketing

I don't want to leave you with the impression that you should adopt a cavalier attitude toward requests made by the marketing team. Every once in a while, they'll ask for something inappropriate, but usually they have sound reasons for their requests. At least that's been my experience.

Sometimes the marketing team will ask for features that aren't strategic for the product from a functional point of view but that are quite strategic for sales reasons. Does any application really need to read and write 23 different file formats, for instance? Of course not; users need only one file format to store their work in. Support for the other 22 formats is driven primarily by marketing needs. If your application isn't "file friendly," that can kill sales, if for no other reason than it discourages users from dumping competing products in favor of yours—they'd lose their preexisting work.

If you're faced with a feature you feel doesn't improve the product, consider whether the feature would measurably increase sales. That *LAYOFF* macro was inappropriate because it would have harmed the product, not because its only reason for being was to land that large corporate account.

If marketers are looking at magazine product-feature checklists, you'll run into the same problem—the requests will be for features that fill out the chart, not for features that are strategically necessary for the product. Sometimes the marketing team will see a questionably useful feature in a competing product and, in a knee-jerk conviction that your product has to do everything that the competitors' products do, ask for the feature. Watch out.

———◆———

Implement features only if they are strategic to the product. Don't implement features merely to fill out feature sets or review checklists.

———◆———

TOTALLY COOL, TECHNICALLY AWESOME

In Chapter 1, I mentioned that the user interface library lead and I reviewed the task list for the library. One of the items on that list was a six-week task to implement a feature that would allow third party vendors to hook little standalone applications into Microsoft's character-based applications. The idea was to make it possible to implement calculators, notepads, clock displays, and other types of desk accessories that Windows and Macintosh users take for granted. I thought the feature was interesting, but it didn't seem to me to be strategic for any of the 20 or so internal groups using the library.

When I asked the lead which group had asked for the feature, he told me that nobody had; it was on the task list because the *previous* lead had felt that it was important. I then asked if any of the groups had expressed interest in the feature when they had learned of it. Again, the lead said he didn't know, and he added that if I was considering cutting the feature, the previous lead would fight it if he found out.

I figured that if the previous lead felt that strongly about supporting desk accessories, there must be groups who really wanted the functionality and that the current lead must simply be unaware of them. So before cutting the feature, we asked the groups if they'd heard of the feature and whether they were interested in such support. The responses we got were all pretty much the same: "Yeah, we heard about that. So and So tried to convince us that it was important."

Most groups didn't want the functionality at all. A few were more interested than others, but only if we beefed up the feature so that there was strong communication between the accessory and the application. They didn't want calculators and clock displays; they wanted the ability to truly extend the application—for grammar checkers and other tools that could provide important functionality. Of course, providing a general purpose interface to allow such functionality was much more complicated than the original idea. We didn't have the time to implement the six-week feature, much less something more complex.

Our findings pretty much killed the feature, but before scratching it off the list, I talked with the previous lead to get his thoughts on the issue. He was disappointed by my decision to cut the feature, but nothing more. He couldn't provide any compelling reasons to implement the code except that it would be an interesting programming challenge and

---

What About Third Party Vendors?

It's possible that third party vendors would have loved to have seen support for those little pop-up applications. It's likely that some small company or enterprising individual would have seized upon that niche market and created numerous little add-ons for Microsoft's character-based applications. Nobody got the chance because I cut the feature. But I didn't cut the feature without first considering how beneficial such third party support might have been.

Had the add-on capability been much more powerful, as the applications groups wanted it to be, third party developers could have created some truly useful add-ons for other users, which in turn could have increased demand for the character-based products. But calculators? Notepads? Clocks? Nobody chooses a word processor, a debugger, or any other application simply because a third party vendor sells a nifty add-on scientific calculator.

Simply put, the users didn't need the functionality, which meant that the applications didn't need it. It would have been wasteful for us to spend six weeks working on pop-up code when we could work on code that users really did care about.

---

that it would have been cool if people could have used the little pop-up applications instead of TSRs, MS-DOS's problematic approach to achieving the same ends.

In effect, what we had was a six-week feature that was not at all strategic to the success of the user interface library, nor to the successes of the applications using the library. The task was on the schedule for only two reasons: it would have been fun to work on, and it would have been cool for the character-based applications to have desk accessories just as their Windows and Macintosh counterparts did.

———◆———

Don't implement features simply
because they are technically challenging
or "cool" or fun or. . .

———◆———

IS IT BETTER?

Sometimes tasks sneak onto the schedule because they seem truly important, but in fact they may not be if you consider whether they are strategic. For example, it has always irritated me that Excel uses a non-standard clipboard paradigm—the clipboard is not persistent. It's not that Excel's model is awkward or less useful; it just bugs me that Excel's clipboard doesn't behave the way clipboards found in every other Macintosh and Windows application behave. The saving grace is that Excel's clipboard implementation is close enough to the standard model that few people ever notice that it's different.

Now, I believe in following standards, particularly those that concern user interfaces. So you can imagine that if I were the Excel lead, I might think it important to bring Excel into line and would therefore put a "standardize the clipboard" task on the schedule. And, in fact, I do think that's important. However, I do not think that standardizing the clipboard is strategic in any way. Changing the clipboard's behavior could also break existing user-defined macros that rely on the current clipboard behavior.

If I were the Excel lead, I would *want* to standardize the clipboard, but I would strike that task from the schedule in an instant. I would feel differently if users were confused or irritated by Excel's clipboard, but as I said, most people never notice that it's different.

Another type of important work that is rarely strategic is reformatting source files to adopt new coding styles or naming conventions. Suppose a project lead decides that all functions must have function headers that describe what the functions do and what the parameters mean. That seems perfectly reasonable. What I question is a lead's taking the next step—bringing development to a halt so that the entire team can spend days or weeks retroactively adding header comments to all the headerless functions written over the years. It's even worse when a lead halts development to institute a new naming convention. That can be incredibly costly if the team stops to rename every existing variable and function name. Such work may be important for maintainability, but it is rarely strategic. You can tell that the work is nonstrategic because it doesn't improve the product in any way.

True, you can view such file reformatting as an investment in maintainability that will ultimately improve the product, but stopping all development is a stiff price to pay. If you ask how you can get the benefits and eliminate the drawbacks, you can derive alternative approaches to adding those header comments all at the same time. An approach could be as simple as asking all programmers to spend half an hour a week writing headers and to add headers to any functions they touch during the day as they work on strategic tasks. Sure, it'll take longer before all the functions have header comments, but such an approach puts the initial investment more in line with the expected return.

Of course, if you're talking about stopping development to add debug code to the product, that might be another matter; adding debug code could definitely improve the quality of the product—and rapidly. The return on investment could be substantial, even in the short term.

Occasionally, I'll run across a Usenet news article in which a programmer says something like "We're in the process of rewriting all of our C code using objects in C++, and I can't figure out how C++ does. . ." When I read such notes, I shudder and hope that those programmers—actually their leads—aren't killing their products by taking the huge time hit that such a rewrite must entail.

You could argue that it would be beneficial to rewrite an assembly language program in a high-level language such as C—the resulting productivity gains could outweigh the costs of doing the rewrite, and the resulting code might be more portable. But I've got to question rewriting a Pascal program in C, or rewriting a C program using object-oriented designs in C++. I suspect that many such rewrites are initiated by leads who get caught up in the hoopla of the latest industry trend. When C++ first started getting attention, there were programmers at Microsoft who wanted to recode anything and everything using object-oriented designs. It didn't matter that the original code worked fine. These programmers felt that it was absolutely necessary to rewrite the existing code. Fortunately, calmer minds prevailed, restricting object-oriented work to new code and to cases in which rewriting a product would provide strategic benefits.

———◆———

Don't waste time on questionable improvement
work. Weigh the potential value returned against
the time you would have to invest.

———◆———

The "Productivity" Cry

The reason I most often heard for rewriting existing C programs in C++ was that the development team would be so much more productive using object-oriented methodologies. That may be true, but the people making those claims were ignoring a significant detail: all the time lost doing the rewrite. Rewriting a C program to use object-oriented designs in C++ is not a line by line translation, as a Pascal to C translation can be; it's a total, ground-up rewrite.

If you're leading multiple groups and one of them comes to you wanting to move from C to C++, ask them whether they're talking about rewriting the application using object-oriented designs, or whether they're simply interested in using the more flexible C++ compiler to compile their existing C code. If they're talking about doing an object-oriented rewrite, be sure to determine whether the benefits would overcome the time lost doing the redesign and rewrite.

Let Nothing Interfere

By now you should have a pretty strong awareness of the kind of work you should be focused on: the strategic work as defined by the project goals. But being focused on strategic work is not enough to prevent schedule slips. You can deflect "free" features, quash the impulse to go after "cool" features, and minimize effort on questionable improvement work. But if you don't learn to say No when you should or if you don't determine what others truly want, you can find yourself drowning in work that you shouldn't be doing.

The key to keeping your projects on track is knowing exactly what you should be doing and then letting nothing interfere with that effort. Of course, the trick is in knowing exactly what you should be doing. That's why it's vital that you create detailed project goals.

Highlights

◆ Don't let foreseeable problems surprise you. If you want your project to run smoothly, take time to look into the future. You can prevent many catastrophes by taking small actions today that either eliminate the problems in the future or steer you clear of them. If you regularly ask the question "What can I do *today* to help keep the project on track for the next few months?" you can determine the actions you need to take.

◆ Before you settle in to solve a problem, be sure you're attacking the right problem. Remember the misguided optimization work the dialog team was doing? The group complaining about the speed problem inadvertently misled the people on the library team. Get to the bottom of the problem before you try to treat it.

◆ Before spending any significant time on a task, do some research so that you know you'll be filling the real need. That request for those bizarre list boxes was misleading because the group really needed hierarchical menus. When you get requests, be sure to find out what it is the askers are trying to accomplish. It can save you lots of time.

◆   For a variety of reasons, some leads find it difficult to say No to demands made on their teams. In the most serious instances, a lead will commit to a ship date knowing the team can't make it. If you have trouble saying No, consider how you'd want groups you're depending on to respond to your own requests. Would you want to know up front that they couldn't make the date on which you need the feature, or would you rather they agreed and then missed that date? Be as responsible to other groups as you would want them to be to yours.

◆   Whenever you get a feature request, determine whether the feature is strategic to the product. If the feature isn't strategic, don't implement it. It doesn't matter that the feature appears to be "free" or that it's technically exciting or that a competitor has it. Especially watch for features that round out a set— such features can appear to be strategically necessary because it feels as though you must include them for completeness. If you're unsure whether a feature is strategic, consider the motivation behind the request for it.

4

*U*NBRIDLED *E*NTHUSIASM

After reading the first three chapters of this book, you might have gotten the impression that I'm one of those leads who likes to keep my team members' noses to the grindstone. I've certainly put enough emphasis on staying focused to justify such a suspicion. But my goal is not to extract the maximum amount of work out of each team member. My goal is to put out a great product that the development team has an exhilarating time putting together.

Have you ever worked on a project that sizzled with enthusiasm? If you haven't, have you at least had single days on which you felt great as you left the office? Think back to such a day. Was it filled with meetings, reports, interviews, and e-mail exchanges, or did you spend the day working uninterrupted, creating great new designs and coding hot new features? We both know the answer. I've never met a programmer who got excited about having written yet another report or having attended yet another meeting.

One of my driving goals as a lead is to create an atmosphere in which the development team can have a blast as they create a product they're proud of. I do that in part by working hard to ensure that programmers don't have to write unnecessary reports, or attend unnecessary meetings, or fuss with schedules, or do anything else that pulls them away from creating new and exciting features for the product. In this chapter, I'll tell you why I think such processes are harmful—as they're commonly practiced—and how you can replace overblown corporate processes that suck the life out of projects with simpler, more effective practices.

THE UNREAD REPORT

Right after I got back from a business trip one time, my lead called me into his office and quizzed me on all the details. When we'd finished talking, he asked me to write up a detailed trip report describing everything I'd just told him. That seemed like a waste of time to me, so I asked if the report was really necessary. He assured me that it was, so I spent the better part of an afternoon writing that report instead of working on features.

Later that month, my lead asked me a question I had fully answered in the trip report. I could understand his not remembering the details, but I was puzzled that he hadn't referred to the report for the answer, so I asked him if he'd read the report. He admitted that he hadn't—he had filed it as soon as I'd given it to him.

"Why did you have me write that report if you never intended to read it?" I was irked.

He gave me a surprised look and said, "*Everybody* has to write trip reports. It's policy. . ."

Any reason he could have offered for having me write the report would have been better than that poor rationale. If he'd had me write the report because studies show that writing something down cements the knowledge better in your head, I could have understood that. If he'd told me he intended to pass the report on to his own lead or to other teams who could benefit from its contents, I could have understood that too. But having me write a report when he knew he was going to file it away unread was absurd. This was an excellent example of somebody's following a guideline as if it were an ironclad rule, and because of it we wound up doing something stupid. Any time corporate policy has somebody writing a report that nobody will read, corporate policy is wrong—unless the ultimate purpose *is* to cement the knowledge better in the writer's head. But if that's the case, do all trips need such cementing? My lead was following business-as-usual, not ruthlessly eliminating all obstacles to product improvement.

The Mystery of the End-Cut Pot Roast

One problem with any process you put in place is that over time people tend to forget the original reason you set up the process, and continue to observe it even though it may be outdated. Somewhere I read a story that succinctly illustrates this point:

> A young boy once asked his mother why she'd cut the ends off a pot roast before she put the roast into the oven. "Well," she said, "because that's what my mother taught me to do." But the question got her to wondering, so she asked her own mother for the reason behind lopping off the ends. "To tell you the truth, I don't know," answered her mother. "I've always done it because that's what I saw your grandmother do." A real mystery. So the boy's mother put the question to her grandmother. Grandma's reply: "Back then, I had a small roasting pan—roasts wouldn't fit into the pan unless I cut off the ends."

Like that boy's mother, the lead who had me write a report he didn't intend to read was following a procedure without understanding its original purpose. Since having me write a report that he knew nobody would read was so clearly a questionable practice, he should have (or I should have) tracked down the idea behind such reports. We might have discovered that not all business trips call for trip reports, and in fact I later found out that they don't.

Some trip reports are definitely worthwhile, particularly the reports people write as soon as they get back from trade shows such as COMDEX. Those reports are typically chock-full of observations and insights about the state of the industry, about what the competition is up to and how the crowds responded to the competition's booths and demonstrations, and about how those same crowds responded to their own company's booths and demonstrations. After a show like COMDEX, trip reports flood e-mail networks. Great stuff.

But not all trip reports provide that kind of value. Just because you flew to Kokomo, Indiana, to isolate a bug at a site there that you couldn't reproduce in your office doesn't mean it's worthwhile to write a trip report when you get back. Would you write a trip report if you had walked down the hall to isolate a problem that showed up only on a tester's machine? I hope not. Would you write a trip report if you had driven across town to isolate a problem that affected a local company? At Microsoft, you wouldn't. You wouldn't even write a trip report if the off-site location were on the opposite side of the state and it had taken you four hours to drive there. But if you took a 20-minute puddle-jumper flight, most managers would ask you to write a trip report. Why? I don't believe the reason has anything to do with whether the report is actually needed. The manager has to fill out special paperwork to authorize the expenditure for the plane ticket. The trip is therefore special, the manager reasons, and requires a report.

When I said that leads should ruthlessly eliminate unnecessary work, the superfluous trip report was the kind of thing I was talking about. Just as I don't call meetings unless the value they provide offsets the interruption they cause, I never ask for a report unless there is a compelling reason for one. I'd much rather have people working on the product and interacting with other team members than working on a report I don't really need. My view is, any time I'm about to interrupt a team member's work, I'd better have a darn good reason—to heck with business-as-usual.

I rarely ask for reports because I don't believe they're worth the disruption they cause. But when I feel I must have a report, my preference is to get an oral report because it takes much less time—5 minutes of interactive communication vs. 30 minutes—or more—of writing.

If you ask some people to write a report, their eyes glaze over. If you drop by three hours later, you're liable to find the person frozen in front of the word processor, having written only two paragraphs. For some people, writing a report ranks right up there with speaking to a full auditorium—it paralyzes them.

Another problem with written reports—if you don't explain exactly what you want—is that people go on at length about stuff you have no interest in. And many people get bogged down in bad prose because they think the text has to "sound like" a report. Instead of writing "the bug showed up only when the floppy drive was empty," such people think they need to say something like "the error occurred only in those instances in which the drive mechanism contained no media." It's harder and takes longer to write in that unnatural style. It's also harder and takes longer to read that kind of writing. Besides, reports written that way are about as exciting as the test pattern on your television set.

When I do ask people to write reports, I ask them to keep the reports as short as possible and to keep the writing informal—to avoid report-speak. I don't demand that they write reports in this style, but I do encourage it. For people who get paralyzed at the prospect of writing a report, these two requests help make it a less painful, less time-consuming affair.

"Keep it as short as possible?" they'll say. "No problem!"

If a team member wants to expand on a few ideas in a written report, that's all right with me too. Some people prefer writing reports over presenting them orally, particularly if they're trying to persuade the reader to act on the contents. A written report can enable both the writer and me to carefully consider exactly what's reported and the line of action the reporter thinks we should take. My goal overall, though, is to get the information I need with the least amount of pain and interruption to the writer.

Written reports, like meetings, interrupt the writer's work. Don't ask for them unless they provide real value—enough to offset the cost of the interruption they cause.

———◆———

Be sure that every report you ask
for is worth the time it takes for the
writer to prepare it.

———◆———

THE GOOD, THE BAD, AND THE SHELVED

One kind of report I have found to be invaluable when it's done well is the project postmortem report. I'm talking about the project analysis some teams write up shortly after a release. A postmortem report answers the question "What can we learn from the project we just finished?" What went right (let's keep doing that) and what went wrong (how can we prevent those problems from recurring in the upcoming project?)? Postmortem reports are crucial because they force the team members to actively consider how they can improve the development process.

I love reading project postmortems because they contain so much good information. But all too often, I'll read a postmortem report that contains important insights but is effectively worthless because the writer hasn't taken the next step: describing exactly what's going to be done about those insights. In one case, I read a pile of postmortems a product team had written over the years. Each report started with "We should have included more debugging code at the start of the project," followed shortly by "We also should have fixed bugs up front instead of allowing them to collect until the end of the project." Both excellent observations. Unfortunately, the same insights appeared in the postmortems for release after release of that product. Apparently, nobody was acting on the team's hard-won knowledge.

If you do postmortem reports—and I advise you to—be sure to include a detailed attack plan that describes how you plan to take care of each known problem so that it doesn't come up again in the next project cycle. I'm sure the team whose pile of postmortems I read never included more debug code at the start of each project or changed their bug-fixing habits. Once the postmortem report was written, they stored it away on some dusty shelf, never to be read again nor acted upon.

Some postmortem reports I've read have contained attack plans, but the plans were ineffective because they weren't specific enough—they had no teeth. Suppose a postmortem report contained this problem and attack plan:

```
Problem: external beta sites felt their bug reports fell
on deaf ears, mainly because the bugs they reported would
continue to appear in beta release after beta release of
our Mandelbrot package. These bugs were slipping through
the cracks because we had no systematic approach for
tracking external bug reports. In the future, we must
try to track external bug reports more carefully.
```

In many cases, that was all the postmortem report would say on the matter. From the occasional team who took the extra step and developed a more specific plan of attack, the plan would look like this:

```
Solution: the Plotting Division needs to implement a
better method for tracking bugs reported by external
beta sites.
```

From the rare team who developed a detailed attack plan, the plan would look like this:

```
Solution: to prevent our losing track of bugs reported
by external beta sites--a problem that affects not
only our Mandelbrot project, but also the Biorhythm and
Morph projects--Hubie Dobson has agreed to review three
well-respected bug-tracking systems (Bug Control, Pro-
grammer's Database, and FixIt!) and recommend one tool
for division-wide use. Hubie will make his recommendation
within the next two weeks (by June 12). We will use the
system Hubie recommends for our Mandelbrot project as
an initial test case, and we will maintain a list of any
tracking problems we encounter.
```

Which of the three reports do you suppose would be most likely to produce change in the development process? The one that states little more than the problem and an intention to do better, the one with a simple attack plan, or the one with the detailed attack plan? Is there any question that the final plan would be the most effective?

The final plan will be the most effective because it tells exactly what the solution will be, who will be responsible, when the deadline is, and where the plan will be applied. The plan also provides for evaluation. Who is accountable in the first or second example? It's easy enough to say, as the second report does, that the Plotting Division should implement a new bug-tracking system, but who is that? And by when should the Plotting Division implement a new method for tracking external bug reports? On which project will they try it out? Will they report the results of the trial? Without such details, attack plans are toothless.

The postmortem report should also describe development practices you found to be worthwhile in the course of the project. The report might say that once the team began using program assertions and debug code, hidden bugs began popping out everywhere, even in code thought to be bug-free. The report might note that the practice of stepping through code in the debugger the moment it is written was at first a bit tedious, but that once programmers got used to the practice the number of bugs found by testers dropped considerably and without hurting the schedule. Or the report might observe that having detailed project goals really helped the team stay focused. These are excellent points. But the report shouldn't stop there.

For each such observation, the postmortem report should indicate how the observation will be exploited in the future. It's not enough that a team discover what works well; they must use that knowledge to its full advantage. If only some team members were habitually stepping through their code the moment they wrote it, for instance, the report might describe the steps that will ensure that all team members will begin to use that bug-finding technique.

Finally, the postmortem should describe as part of its attack plan some method for making the findings in the report available to other teams. This part of the attack plan could be as simple as saying "we will provide copies of this report to the following leads by such and such a date." That plan tells what, who, and when.

Researching and writing postmortem reports takes time and adds yet more process to development—which I oppose on principle—but the educational benefits of postmortem reports compensate for the time deficit, with one caveat: you must act on your findings. If postmortem reports end up on the shelf, never to be read again, they haven't been worth doing.

By the way, you don't need to wait for the end of a full release cycle to write a postmortem report. Every time you run into a problem or discover a better way of doing things, jot your findings down in an ongoing document and take immediate action to exploit your new knowledge. Why wait until you've shipped to gain the benefits?

———◆———

Use postmortem reports to improve your development process. To make a report effective, describe exactly how your team plans to fix known problems and how it plans to exploit the effective development practices it has discovered.

———◆———

MEETINGS TO MISS

In Chapter 1, I talked about why I think weekly status meetings are unnecessary if you're already collecting status reports of some kind. But status meetings are just one form of the recurrent meeting, a kind of meeting I routinely try to eradicate. By "recurrent meeting" I mean any regularly scheduled gathering. You arrive at work, week in and week out, and you think, "It's Tuesday. I'd better not forget that regular three o'clock meeting."

I rarely hold meetings because they can be so disruptive to the smooth flow of work, and I particularly dislike recurring meetings because the motivation for holding such meetings usually isn't clear. Are you meeting because you need to, or because it's three o'clock Tuesday? Some people would argue that weekly status meetings are indispensable. I've gone without them for years. It's not the meeting that's important; it's the information you would get by attending such a meeting. If you can get (or pass on) the status information more efficiently without a meeting, why not take that approach? As I said in Chapter 1, my teams' little "I've just finished. . ." e-mail notes have worked fine for me.

Does it ever make sense to hold meetings? Of course. There are times when meetings do more good than harm. In particular, meetings can be valuable when

◆   one individual must pass information on to a large number of other people and a meeting is the most efficient way to do that

◆   people must be able to actively respond to information—to ask questions or to interact with other attendees

◆   value will be realized from seeing or experiencing something—a product demonstration, for instance

◆ a matter too delicate for a memo or an e-mail—a reorganization or layoffs, for example—must be discussed

A meeting doesn't need to meet all of these criteria in order to be worthwhile—any one of them will do, provided there isn't a better alternative. In the days of stone tablets and parchment scrolls, it made sense to hold meetings to pass out information—that was the most efficient method. You gathered the masses and did the "Hear ye, hear ye" bit. But today, with photocopiers, electronic mail, and electronic bulletin boards, you can pass out information with much greater efficiency, and without interrupting people's work. Of course, you should use common sense. If you have something important to say, holding a meeting to say it underscores the importance and guarantees that everyone will hear the message. And if you're a dynamic speaker, you can rally attendees to action.

Before you call any meeting, take a minute to ask these questions:

Will the results of this meeting be important enough to warrant interrupting the work of the people who will have to attend it?

Is there a less disruptive way I can get the results I'd get from holding the meeting?

Team Spirit

I've heard some leads say that their weekly status meetings are important because the meetings get the entire team into one room where they can see each other face-to-face. The practice builds team spirit, they say. I've heard of leads who hold status meetings *primarily* so that the team members can get together. The objective is a good one, but in my experience, the status meeting is just about the worst venue for promoting team spirit. If your status meetings are like the ones I've described, in which the focus is on what everybody *didn't* get done that week, such status meetings won't really help build team spirit.

If your team members don't tend to meet often in spontaneous hall gatherings and brainstorming sessions, maybe you do need to create opportunities for mingling. If that's the goal, go out for group lunches, or schedule some other *positive* activity together. Forget using those punishing status meetings for that purpose.

When you ask these questions about a prospective design meeting, you can see that it probably does make sense to interrupt the team's work, or at least the work of part of the team. The work done at a design meeting improves the product. It directly influences how the product will be built. The team may be getting pulled from their individual tasks, but they're still focused on the product, not on housekeeping. Design meetings also encourage rapid-fire debate over the trade-offs among various designs. You can't easily or efficiently brainstorm that way over e-mail.

I would be suspicious, though, of any design meeting that was regularly held at three o'clock every Tuesday. Unless you have scheduled a series of specific design tasks—design the memory manager this Tuesday, the file I/O next Tuesday, the internal document structure the Tuesday after that, and so on—I doubt that a regular design meeting makes sense. I'd imagine that a recurring design meeting would always open with the question "Have any new design issues cropped up this week?" And I'd like to assume that if such issues had cropped up, they wouldn't have been kept quiet until the next Tuesday. Team members should bring up new design issues immediately, and if a gathering

---

Good Meeting Times

If you must have a meeting, at least schedule it so that it doesn't break up an otherwise large chunk of time. Don't schedule your one-hour meeting at 10:00 A.M. or 3:00 P.M. so that it chops the morning or the afternoon into two-hour pieces. Schedule the meeting at the beginning or the end of the day, or just before or right after lunch. In other words, schedule your meetings next to standard break times to maximize the size of uninterrupted time blocks.

Another approach is to schedule all your weekly meetings in one continuous block—say, on Monday morning or Friday afternoon. Monday morning and Friday afternoon are notoriously the least productive times of the work week anyway. Put all your meetings into one of those blocks of time, and keep them out of the better, more productive, parts of the week.

---

seems necessary to work out problems, you can call an ad hoc meeting. Reserving a time each week "just in case" there are problems seems to me to be more disruptive than helpful.

---◆---

Beware of recurrent meetings. Make sure
they're worth the disruption they cause.

---◆---

EFFECTIVE MEETINGS

As much as I dislike holding meetings, or attending other people's meetings, I recognize that meetings are sometimes necessary. And as for any unpleasant task I believe is necessary, I ask the benefits-drawbacks question: How can I get the benefits of this meeting without the drawbacks?

The benefits of meetings are the results you get out of those meetings, and the chief drawback is that so many meetings are a waste of time because there aren't any results—often because the purpose of a meeting was never clear to the participants. You can hold a far more effective meeting if you first decide exactly what you want to accomplish at the meeting and then come up with a plan to get those results by meeting's end. It's the old "set your goals and create an attack plan" scenario.

Once you've decided that a meeting is necessary, be sure to ask this question before you send out the invitations:

What do I expect to achieve at this meeting, and how can I be sure
to achieve it?

If you ask this question before each meeting, you have a much better chance of not wasting everybody's time with random presentation and discussion.

Remember that hypothetical house-moving lead I talked about in Chapter 3, the one who didn't drive ahead to check out the route before the house hit the road? The driver ran into overpasses, hills, and roadwork because the lead didn't take the steps beforehand that would have ensured they could get the results they wanted.

When you ask yourself what you expect to achieve at a meeting, you force yourself to look ahead for possible obstacles to what you hope to achieve and to take steps to avoid them. If you have a clear idea of what you want to achieve and of what is necessary to achieve it, you can see that all key decision makers attend and that they bring whatever you'll need for the results you want. How many meetings have been for naught simply because a key decision maker couldn't attend, or because somebody didn't know to bring a vital piece of information?

Still, despite your best efforts, there will be times when you won't have all the information you need to make a final decision. When that happens, the meeting coordinator will often say something like "George, find out if your two-week guesstimate for the Anagram feature is accurate, and we'll meet again to decide whether to include it in this release."

Leads who use that approach waste people's time. Everybody met, yet nothing was decided. If your goal is to get a decision, *make sure you get a decision*, even if it's a conditional one. It's far better to end a meeting with, "Assuming that George's guesstimate for the Anagram feature is accurate, does everybody agree that this feature is strategic enough to delay our WordSmasher ship date?"

With that question, you may find that nobody thinks the feature is strategic enough to jeopardize the ship date. Or maybe that they think the feature is so important it doesn't matter how it affects the ship date. But more often than not, you can get a conditional decision: "Let's do it, provided the Anagram feature won't delay the ship date by more than two weeks."

Such a decision may not be as concrete as a definite Yea or Nay, but it's infinitely preferable to postponing the resolution of the issue and calling yet another meeting. If your goal is to get a decision, *get one*. If your goal is to achieve something else, make sure you achieve that.

———◆———

*Before calling any meeting, be sure you
know exactly what you want to achieve
and what you need to achieve it. Then
make sure you* do *achieve it.*

———◆———

A Metric for Meetings

I've hammered on the idea of getting decisions at your meetings because almost every worthwhile meeting ends with a decision of some kind. If you hold a meeting that doesn't end in a decision, that meeting has probably been a waste of time.

Think about a status meeting. Is it held to reach a decision? No, its purpose is to pass information around. What about a design meeting? Yes, you're deciding on a design for the product. The meeting may be a brainstorming session, but the goal is to leave the meeting with a design, or at least a design approach, that everybody agrees on.

What about an upper management project review meeting? Can it end with a decision? That depends. I've seen two types. In the first, the lead describes the course of the project over the last year, touching on major highlights, and finishes by reviewing the current schedule and expressing some level of confidence about the projected dates. In the second type of project review meeting, the lead doesn't dawdle over the past but instead describes in detail where she is taking the project, why she has chosen that direction, what her detailed attack plan is, what the alternative approaches that she rejected were and why she rejected them, how her plan fits into the long-term direction of the company, and finally how upper management can help—all she needs is their support.

The first type of review meeting is just dumping information on upper management, whereas the second type is a presentation to persuade upper management to back the lead's plan, to get them to *decide* to support her plan. Which type of presentation do you think is better for the company, getting upper management to focus on the past or getting them to commit to a course for the future?

Some gatherings, such as pep rallies and the annual company meeting, don't result in decisions, but those meetings have a different purpose, and more important, they aren't held each week, or even each month.

No Follow-Up Work

Another drawback to meetings is that they tend to create follow-up tasks for the people who attend. Sometimes you can't do without a follow-up task—you need to have George figure out exactly how long it would take to implement that Anagram feature in WordSmasher—but a lot of follow-up work is busywork. Remember the lead who required team members to send follow-up e-mail repeating what they'd said at the meeting? Follow-up work is just that much more work that pulls the development team away from the tasks they were doing before the meeting started.

Whenever you're wrapping up a meeting, restating the decisions you've reached and recounting the action items for various attendees, be sure to consider whether each follow-up action item is essential. I know several leads who seem to feel that everybody must have picked up at least one action item by the end of a meeting. Such a lead will circle the table mentioning what each person is to do—until he hits upon somebody with no follow-up task. He'll stop for a minute, scratch his head, and manufacture a task: "George, why don't you. . ."

If you've fallen into this tendency, try a different approach. As you circle the table, reevaluate each action item to determine whether it's really worth spending time on. A typical dialogue might go like this:

"Next is George. You were going to get an estimate for the Anagram feature. Realistically, do you think there's any possibility of doing that feature without affecting the ship date by more than two weeks?"

"Actually, I've thought of some additional issues in the last 20 minutes," George says. "I now think the feature will take at least three weeks to implement."

"OK. The Anagram feature isn't important enough to jeopardize our ship date, so let's postpone the feature until the 3.1 release. Everybody agree? Good. George, you have no action items. Now, Rebecca, you were going to. . ."

I think you'll be surprised at how many follow-up tasks don't seem nearly as important by the end of the meeting as they did earlier, in the middle of an intense discussion.

Try to eliminate unnecessary
follow-up work.

Wriggling Out Of Work

Doesn't circling the table looking for ways to eliminate work create a harmful negative feedback loop, one that encourages people to misinform you so that they'll get out of some work? Did George really find another week's worth of work when he looked again at doing the Anagram feature, or did he fabricate that week's worth of work as a means of getting the feature killed—and reducing his work load?

In any organization, you're going to find some individuals who have no qualms about lying to ease their burdens. That's life. But I believe the vast majority of people are sincere and don't play such games. You quickly find out who the other few are.

Besides, I doubt that a team would so easily kill a feature (or an action item) if they felt it was important. That Anagram feature would not have been dropped if the others at the meeting had felt it was strategic to the current release.

BREAK OUT THE JACKHAMMER

If you want to keep the excitement level in your team high, enable them to work on the product without constantly being pulled off their work to write reports, attend meetings, and deal with other processes that won't help to improve the product. Unfortunately, the corporate tendency is to call meetings for every little thing and to ask for reports as a knee-jerk reaction: "I'm busy right now; send me a report."

You might think that a little speed bump in the road would be just a small obstacle, but imagine how such a bump would affect a race car going at a high speed—it could break the car apart. The development team is like that race car, raring to go, and just as they start to pick up speed, WHUMP, they hit a speed bump in the form of a meeting, a report, or some other corporate process. Sometimes it's worse. The lead who regularly asked for status reports, called status meetings, and required follow-up reports was a one-man speed-bump builder. WHUMP, WHUMP, WHUMP. . .

You may not have control over all the speed bumps that slow your team, but you certainly have control over many of them. Retire that truck full of blacktop and break out your jackhammer. Do some real damage to those bumps.

HIGHLIGHTS

◆   Try to limit the number of reports you ask other team members to write. Be sure that every report you ask for will provide more value to you or the company than would be lost by interrupting the writer's work.

◆   Postmortem reports are invaluable when you do them correctly. Unless your postmortem reports explain exactly how you intend to fix known problems or exploit known improvements, though, the reports probably aren't worth doing.

◆   Before you call a meeting, be sure the results you think you'll get from that meeting are worth the disruption to the work of the people who would have to attend. Be particularly wary of any regular meeting. Regular, standing meetings often aren't worth the time to walk to them, much less attend.

◆   If you must hold a meeting, minimize the amount of interruption it will cause. Schedule the meeting so that it won't break up an otherwise large block of time.

◆   Whenever you call a meeting, be sure you know ahead of time exactly what you're trying to accomplish, and then make sure you do accomplish it. Remember also that conditional decisions are better than no decisions.

5

SCHEDULING MADNESS

I explained in Chapter 2 why I believe it's critical that teams fix bugs as they're found. We didn't follow that practice back when I was working on the Microsoft Excel project. In fact, we were pressured to ignore bugs until all scheduled features had been completed. Why? Because if we had stopped to fix bugs we would have appeared to have slipped the schedule. It wouldn't have mattered that the ship date would actually have been pulled in; anything that appeared to cause intermediate slips was discouraged, and a growing bug-list didn't count as slipping— you'd slipped only if you hadn't "finished" a feature as scheduled. The schedule, not the project goals and priorities, not even common sense, was driving the development process.

At that time, Microsoft's Applications division used a type of schedule that seemed reasonable on paper but that in practice demoralized teams and created a situation in which the strongest motive was to hit deadlines at the expense of all else—including product quality. Of course, at the time nobody thought of it that way because the problems weren't apparent. It took Microsoft several years—a round of product cycles for its applications—to realize the problems inherent in the scheduling system it was using.

Once the problems with the scheduling system became apparent, the process was tossed out, and a more humane scheduling system was brought in. Still, that was a costly learning experience for Microsoft, and I'll describe that experience so that others don't follow the same mistaken path. I'll also describe the scheduling process that many groups at Microsoft have moved to and that I have found to work quite well.

On a Project Long, Long Ago. . .

My primary reason for joining Microsoft back in 1986 was to work on high-quality Macintosh applications. I was assigned to Microsoft Excel, then Microsoft's latest entry into the Macintosh market. By any measure, working on Excel should have been exciting for me. It met all of my criteria: it was a serious Macintosh application, it was a highly visible application, and users loved it. Even better, Microsoft wasn't about to go belly-up, so I knew that the product would have a long life. I could get the Macintosh experience I wanted and have an influence on one of the industry's most promising applications.

Working on Excel was exciting at first, but after several months the work had become dull and then finally just plain aggravating. The Excel project should have been a dream project. It didn't make sense that I should find it so aggravating, but other team members were aggravated too, and so were programmers I knew who were working on other Microsoft projects. The problem wasn't the people we worked with, nor was it the work setting—Microsoft's environment was the best I'd experienced, hands down, in 10 years of computer industry work, and I know the aggravated team members and programmers on other Microsoft projects felt that way too. No, the aggravation was a side effect of the type of project schedules Microsoft had begun using right around the time I joined up.

In the projects I'd worked on before I joined Microsoft, the team members had been excited by the work, and the dominant feeling had been enthusiasm over how much better the product was getting with each passing day. The Excel project never felt that way. Although we regularly improved the product, we were bombarded perpetually with the message that we were slipping. I was slipping, he was slipping, *everybody* was slipping, *the project was slipping!* The focus wasn't on the quality or even the quantity of our work: it was on the schedule.

In Chapter 1, I mentioned weekly status reports that had the effect of regularly slapping the programmers in the face. Those reports were just one aspect of the demoralizing scheduling process Microsoft was using back then. Besides writing those weekly status reports, the team members had to meet each week with the testing and documentation teams for a general discussion of how we'd slipped that week. We'd learn that the writers were stopped cold because the programmers had slipped and that the testers were sitting on their hands because the programmers had slipped. All we talked about was slipping.

I think even worse than the status reports and those awful status meetings was the project task list. Each week the Excel lead would use the latest round of status reports to update the master task list. Then he'd distribute the updated master list to each team member. Nothing wrong with that. But the first item you'd notice on the cover page would be the chart showing exactly how much each team member had slipped that week and how much the project as a whole had slipped. The chart didn't explain that you'd slipped because you'd had to tackle several unlisted but nevertheless required tasks that hadn't been anticipated back when the schedule had been created. Upper management would get these reports, see that you'd slipped yet again, and demand to know what was going on. Slap! Slap! Slap! It was not pretty in those days.

After the sting had lessened a bit, you'd turn to subsequent pages of the master task list and see what seemed like thousands of unfinished items. Worse, the list would be almost identical to the one you'd seen the week before. Here we were, working our hardest, and almost nothing seemed to be getting done. It was like that joke, "How do you eat an elephant? . . . A bite at a time." The task list was our elephant, and it seemed as if we'd never finish eating it.

The focus was so much on the schedule's deadline that no matter how solid our work was we couldn't feel any sense of accomplishment. Quite the contrary: we were overwhelmed by the feeling we were so far behind that even with our best efforts we couldn't make any headway. It wasn't the nature of the work that was the problem; it was the apparent hopelessness of the position we were in.

Until that Excel project, I'd never seen how destructive a schedule can be to morale. What should have been my dream job felt like a nightmare. We were constantly slipping our schedule, but we weren't goofing off. The reality was that the project's schedule was hopelessly unrealistic. The schedule made these assumptions, for instance:

- That all tasks—for a two-year project—were known and listed on the schedule

- That each week each programmer would complete 40 hours' worth of the tasks listed on the schedule

- That all task estimates were completely accurate

- That all features would be implemented perfectly, without bugs

The world's most accomplished programming team couldn't have met a schedule based on those assumptions—unless, that is, they had regularly worked 80-hour weeks from the outset to compensate for all the unforeseen tasks, inaccurate estimates, and bugs, to say nothing of the meetings, reports, interviews, and e-mail that steal hours each week. The schedule also failed to account for the 10 legal holidays each year and for each programmer's two-week vacation each year. For a two-year project, that was an *almost-two-team-months* scheduling error. The schedule was doomed to slip.

———◆———

Never allow the schedule to drive the
project or to demoralize the team.

———◆———

Just Following Standard Procedure

I want to emphasize that the Excel lead didn't intend to create a demoralizing situation. He was following the accepted scheduling process, and he later even adjusted the 40-hours-per-week assumption to account for meetings and other regular but unscheduled tasks—something that some leads on other projects would never do. Nor do I believe the schedule was intentionally designed to extract 80-hour work weeks from the programmers, although that was the result and is perhaps the source of Microsoft's reputation for working people hard. I believe the schedule was a sincere attempt to accurately predict and track progress. After all, what makes more sense than using the sum of the estimates for all known tasks to derive a scheduled "done date"? Of course, nobody believed the task list was complete or that all the estimates were accurate, but that didn't stop people—particularly upper management—from treating the derived "done date" as though it were realistic. In time, most Microsoft groups scrapped these task-list–driven schedules for a type of schedule that was more successful and that I'll describe later in the chapter.

PRIMING THE PUMP

You've probably heard at least one lead say, "If you want the team to work hard, you have to give them an aggressive schedule." I think all leads believe that to some degree—I certainly do. The question is, how aggressive is "aggressive"? If *aggressive* means making the schedule challenging enough that it drives the project forward at a reasonable clip, that's fine; but if *aggressive* means *unattainable*, such a schedule can only demoralize the team as slip-hysteria sets in.

A schedule should be aggressive enough to instill a sense of urgency in the programmers, to help them stay more focused on the important work. Think about your own situation. If you were taking off for a three-week vacation tomorrow, would you work at the same pace today that you normally would? My guess is that you'd work much smarter today than you usually do. You'd probably focus squarely on getting all high-priority items out of the way—no long chats in the halls, no time spent on unimportant e-mail or news, no unnecessary meetings. That's the sense of urgency in action—better focus.

At Microsoft, the same sense of urgency develops whenever a final ship date nears. The lead typically sends out an e-mail message similar to this one:

```
We're nearing our ship date, so we need to be particu-
larly careful about how we use our time. Everybody's time
is valuable now--we're all working toward this one final
goal. Think twice before calling a meeting. Think twice
before bothering somebody with a question you could
easily look up yourself. If you come across an unexpected
task, don't assume that somebody else is going to take
care of it; they're just as busy as you are. Don't keep
a private to-do list of tasks that you'll get around to
"eventually." There is no "eventually." Tell me about
every pending task so that we can decide whether the task
is critical for this release. If you find yourself with
nothing to do, don't kick back because you think you're
done. Unless the team is done, you're not done. I could
go on, but you're all smart. You've all got brains. You
know if you're wasting time.
```

Whenever I see a notice like this one (they get passed to other groups periodically), my question is, shouldn't the team be working that way *all* the time?

"Geez, Steve, that sounds pretty awful. I thought you said in the last chapter that you weren't a 'nose to the grindstone' kind of lead." I'm not. If you look at the essence of that message, you'll see that it says, "Don't do business-as-usual. Work smarter-than-usual. Question every task to prevent wasting time, be careful about wasting other people's time, and take an active role in moving the product forward." That's what I've been saying all along. The language in the e-mail is harsh because the lead wants to convey in one message what I've had the luxury of spending a few chapters on.

If you felt pressed for time, would you conclude a meeting with "George, find out about such and such, and we'll meet again to make a final decision"? I doubt it. When people are pressed for time, they don't put tasks off—they either kill those tasks or handle them immediately.

Do you think a team would crackle with energy if they didn't have a sense of urgency? Imagine a team with so much time to spare that they could arrive each morning, put their feet up, and mull over every aspect of their project. Such contemplation can be rewarding, and the findings can certainly be valuable, but would the team be filled with energy and enthusiasm? Would the project be exciting? Somehow I doubt it, just as I doubt that a slow exchange of ideas can be as exciting as a rapid-fire brainstorming session. I believe that for a team to get on a creative roll, you have to pump energy into the process. The sense of urgency—time pressure—is one source of that energy.

———◆———

Make sure your schedules are attainable
but aggressive enough to keep team members
focused on steady progress.

———◆———

HOW MUCH IS TOO MUCH?

Can you pump too much urgency into a situation? Sure. If the schedule starts to look unattainable, you risk having team members start to make stupid decisions. I've worked with programmers who felt so swamped they stopped testing their code. If the code compiled and didn't blow up the first time they ran it, they moved on. Those programmers knew they weren't doing quality work, but they felt they had no choice, given the pressure of the schedule. They crossed their fingers and prayed that the testing team would catch any bugs that slipped through.

As a lead, you must keep your eye on the decisions people make under schedule pressure and remind people, when you have to, that hitting the deadline is rarely so critical that they should jeopardize the product with ill-conceived designs, slapped-together implementations, or untested code. Missing a deadline will hurt the project once, but bad designs and implementations will haunt the product forever—unless someone further down the line decides to use valuable time to rewrite all the sloppy code.

———◆———

Never allow team members to jeopardize
the product in the attempt to hit what might
be, after all, an arbitrary deadline.

———◆———

THE WIN-ABLE SCHEDULE

A win-able schedule is one that benefits both the company and the developer. As I've pointed out, the schedule must be aggressive enough to get the product out the door but attainable enough to allow the developers to feel they have time to do what you and they believe is best for the product. Another essential aspect of a win-able schedule is that it emphasize the progress made by the team, creating situations in which the team can have "wins."

Do you remember that elephantine Excel task list I talked about earlier in this chapter, the one that stayed the same size from week to week? For almost two years I would routinely arrive at work each day and knock a few tasks off that huge list. How much urgency do you think I felt as I chipped away at features for a deadline two years away? I can tell you: not much. In fact, the project didn't begin to feel urgent until practically the last couple of months, when the deadline was in plain sight.

Maybe you've heard the saying that a goal without a deadline is just a wish. It's the deadline that pumps energy into the development effort and gets people to scrap the dreary procedures of business-as-usual in favor of more effective strategies. We had a deadline for the Excel project, but that deadline was so far out that it had no power to ignite the team. We might as well have said, "Someday we'll ship Excel."

Without exception, every exciting project I've worked on has had deadlines much closer than Excel's two-year release date. It's not that the projects weren't large and didn't undergo development over a long period of time—they were and they did—but they were broken up into smaller subprojects, each with its own deadline, and the deadlines were spaced roughly two months apart. The result was that each subproject had an attainable near-term deadline that promoted the sense of urgency and each contributed to our feeling of progress as we completed it. We didn't ship every two years. We "shipped" every two months.

Thankfully, most Microsoft teams have moved to some form of this milestone-scheduling since the days when I worked on that Excel project. But using milestone-scheduling isn't enough. If you were to take

Arbitrary Deadlines

In my experience, most deadlines are arbitrary, either derived from the list of known tasks or simply handed down from above: "Thou shalt ship on June 11, or else." If you agree to a deadline, you should try to hit it, but the fact that you or upper management has set a date doesn't mean that the date is a priority that overrides quality. The date is too arbitrary. Think about your own project. If you missed the ship date by a month, what would the long-term impact on the company be? Would anyone even care six months later? But suppose, instead, that you hit your deadline and shipped your code with bugs and ill-conceived features. Which would affect your product more, a slightly late release date or an onslaught of bad product reviews?

Unless your code has to be functional by a date that simply can't be changed—say, the arrival of Halley's Comet after a long 76 years—your release date is probably not so critical that you must hit it at all costs. If your not having a piece of equipment ready for a scheduled space shuttle launch would cost your company millions of dollars, it would probably be better to cut functionality and focus on getting all the bugs out of the remaining code than to send all the code aloft and have the equipment crash the first time the astronauts try to use it.

Of course, this discussion makes it sound as if it takes more time to do things right. In my experience, it takes *less* time to do something the right way. You do spend more time up front as you set goals and priorities, think through designs and implementations, create test suites, and set quality bars, but you save a lot of time later. Think about it. Which would be more valuable, writing test suites at the start of the project or at the very end? It's that simple. When other teams are working 80-hour weeks, scrambling to whittle down their huge bug-lists, your team can have almost no bugs and spend the last few weeks of the project cycle adding ever more thorough checks to the test suites and debug code just to find that one, last, unknown bug.

Excel's two-year task list and merely chop it into two-month chunks, you wouldn't change anything—you'd still have a two-year schedule, but now with artificial "ship" dates every two months. It's not the two-month period alone that creates the wins and fosters enthusiasm. It's the thrill of finishing an interesting subproject.

"Finishing all top-priority items" may be important, but the top-priority items don't make up a subproject. They're just a random list of things that happen to be important. There's no motivating theme behind such a list.

"Implementing the charting subsystem" is a subproject. All of the tasks that would be involved would relate to that common theme. You might use a task list to remind people of the known charting issues they'd have to handle, but ultimately the theme of the subproject would drive development. The goal wouldn't be for the team to finish 352 unrelated tasks. The goal would be to do everything necessary to fully complete—to "ship"—the charting subsystem, regardless of whether the tasks it would take were on a list somewhere. The subproject would be in "ship mode" from the outset.

Think of it this way: if you were throwing a dinner party and you went to the store for groceries, would you search only for the party items you'd thought to write down on your shopping list, or would you view that list as the "known items" you need for the party and walk the store aisles thinking "What else do I need? What have I forgotten? There must be something I haven't thought of. . ." Wouldn't you also have a sense of urgency? That's the difference between trying to fulfill a goal—"Get everything I need for my party"—and merely checking off items on a list of unrelated tasks.

Remember that typical e-mail message from the lead as a ship date nears? The emphasis is on wrapping everything up, especially all loose ends. When people focus on a task list, the question they ask themselves is "What's next on my list?" When they focus on a subproject, the question is usually quite different: "What else needs to get done?" The focus is on searching out and handling every task related to the subproject.

Any milestone without a theme ends up having to be driven by a task list because, without a theme, you need such a list in order to know what you're supposed to do.

---◆---

Break long-term projects into shorter,
well-defined subprojects.

---◆---

The Wow! Factor

One way to view the difference between improving the product with unrelated high-priority tasks and completing specific subprojects is to look at your house as if you were going to remodel it. Which updates would have more impact: newly painted trim in one room, a new light fixture in another, a new end table in the living room, and so on, or the living room completely transformed—new paint, new carpet, new furniture, and new art on the walls? When you release a subproject, you get the "living room effect." Internal users, beta testers, upper management—in fact, everybody who fires up the code—thinks Wow! when they see what's been done. With the incremental task list approach, people notice a change here, a change there, but nothing major. That's not bad, but why settle for low impact when you could get more?

Of course, the only difficulty lies in choosing subprojects that present enough different aspects of the work that programmers won't be stumbling over each other, all needing to work on the same source file. I've never found this to be a difficult problem to solve, though.

Eliciting a Wow! can be a critical catalyst that gets a team going on a creative roll.

ENHANCING THE WOW! EFFECT

A milestone goal such as "Finish all top-priority items" is just a mishmash of probably unrelated items. If the ship date for such a subproject were threatened, the lead would be able to mask the problem by quietly reprioritizing the tasks. That might allow the lead to look better, but it would be a misleading and questionable way to go about things.

A more coherent milestone theme would be "Complete all features that affect the visual display so that we can finalize screen shots for the user manual." This milestone is better because it has a theme that's easy to grasp and because it's easy to judge which tasks are appropriate. You can point to any known task and instantly determine whether it affects the visual display. Even better, if an unforeseen task crops up midway through the milestone period, anybody on the team, no matter how green, can easily determine whether it needs to be tackled or whether it can be postponed until work on an appropriate subproject begins.

Often you can attack a major project in any of several ways. Use that latitude to create subprojects that will result in exciting conclusions, to get that Wow! effect. When we were working on the Macintosh C/C++ cross development system, I broke the job up into these subprojects:

- Isolate all Intel 80x86–specific code in the compiler to enable support for other processor types.

- Implement a bare-bones MC680x0 code generator in the compiler.

- Implement MC680x0 assembly listing support in all tools.

- Implement MC680x0 object file support in all tools.

- Link a single-segment application, and run it.

- Link a multi-segment application, and run it.

- Add code optimizations to the code generator.

- . . .

I chose these specific milestones and a few more because each, according to my estimation, would take around one to two months to complete, each was easy to understand, and, with the exception of isolating the Intel 80x86 code, each had an exciting conclusion. Don't think we didn't hoot and holler the first time we had code generation working or when we first saw the generated code dumped on the screen in proper assembly language format. We cheered when we linked and ran our first test application and especially when, after adding some basic optimizations, we realized that the compiler was already generating code comparable to code from the two leading Macintosh compilers on the market.

It was exciting!

Don't Forget the Details

Of course, none of the milestone descriptions was as simple as the one-liners for the cross development system. "Link a single-segment application and run it" doesn't provide enough detail. The actual milestone statement was more specific:

> We should be able to copy an arbitrary single-file Macintosh program into a build directory, rename the file *test.c*, and type *make*. The program should compile without problems, the object files should link without problems, and the executable should transfer automatically to the Macintosh over a cable that connects the Macintosh with the development machine. Then, on the Macintosh, we should be able to double-click on the new file and run the code without problems.

From this more detailed description, you can see that we had to handle all the loose ends in the compiler project, including support for the Macintosh-specific C-language extensions such as \p Pascal strings, Pascal-compatible calling conventions for use in call-back routines, ROM traps, 4-character *long*s for resource types, and so on. We had to modify the 80x86 linker to support MC680x0 code and to create Macintosh-formatted executables. We had to write the runtime startup code, some C library code, and the code to support the transfer mechanism between the PC development machine and the target Macintosh. There was a lot of stuff to do.

You won't always achieve such aggressive milestone goals. We didn't for this particular milestone, but we came close. Supporting some of the Macintosh C-language extensions required changes to the front end of the compiler, and a different team was in charge of that code. At the time, they were frantically putting the final touches on their own release and didn't have time enough to do that work, much less ours, nor did they want us mucking around in their code. We got those changes after their release. You take what you can get.

I could have organized the project so that all high-priority work was done first, followed by secondary work, and so on, but the sub-projects would have been quite different, and they almost certainly wouldn't have been accompanied by the Wow! effect.

To keep the subprojects challenging (and realistic), we didn't use a simple "hello world" test application. That would hardly have exercised the compiler, the linker, and the other tools. We used a small but fully functional public domain Macintosh program. Because we used a real application, we not only saw that the compiler was truly viable but were also forced to handle numerous final-detail issues that a simpler program wouldn't have raised. In task list scheduling, handling such details would have been relegated to the end of the whole project, but the thought of seeing the real-life Macintosh application run spurred the team on, and what could have been boring final-detail work later turned into work we *wanted* to do—and quickly.

Granted, it can be quite disturbing to your lead if he or she doesn't understand that you're using this thematic method of scheduling. It will seem as though you're throwing darts to choose which tasks to do rather than picking the highest-priority tasks.

——◆——

*To foster creative rolls, make sure
that each subproject results in an
exciting conclusion.*

——◆——

THE BEST-CASE DATE

People often forget that the purpose of the schedule is to estimate a completion date given the tasks known at the time. Such a date is not a commitment in the sense that you must hit it at all costs; rather, the date is a good-faith estimate of when the known tasks could be done, with the understanding that there are usually plenty of unknown tasks. In short, the schedule predicts a *best-case* ship date, not *the* ship date. That may not be what upper management wants to hear, but it's reality. Using milestone scheduling instead of task-list–driven scheduling helps to bring the best-case date in line with a realistic ship date, but milestone scheduling isn't perfect either.

As a lead, you must protect your product by emphasizing to your team that product quality is more important than hitting an arbitrary deadline. Remember the lesson from this chapter:

The surest way to mismanage a project and jeopardize the product is to put so much emphasis on the schedule that it demoralizes the team and drives them to make stupid decisions despite their better judgments.

I certainly believe that you should try to hit every deadline you commit to, but keep that "best-case date" idea in mind. That way, if you find yourself about to make a bad decision just to hit that best-case date, maybe you'll stop yourself before any serious damage can be done.

HIGHLIGHTS

◆   The schedule can have a devastating effect on a project if it creates slip-hysteria and causes team members to make bad trade-offs in order to hit arbitrary deadlines. If you create a schedule that has unattainable goals—in hopes of extracting as much overtime as you can get out of each developer—you're creating a situation that will demoralize the team. Once the team members feel they're in a hopeless position, you're going to get anything but optimum work from them, and once the project is finished—maybe sooner—they're going to look elsewhere for work.

◆   By using project milestones instead of task lists to schedule, you can shift the focus to completing subprojects, which creates "wins" for the team and emphasizes progress. If you space the milestones at roughly two-month intervals, you can create a sense of urgency that will help people stay focused, particularly if the milestones have strong, exciting themes. Try to create milestone subproject goals that result in the team's thinking "Wow! Look at what we've accomplished!" As they reach successive milestones, the team will have a growing sense that their work is important and that they're doing something valuable for the product's users. That sense of contribution and the sense of value created can have a remarkable influence, making a team pull together to put out a great product—and have a blast doing it.

6

CONSTANT, UNCEASING IMPROVEMENT

During this year's Winter Olympic Games, I was struck by one aspect of the figure skating events. The television footage of earlier gold medal performances seemed to suggest that 25 years ago you could win a gold medal with a few layback and sit spins, a couple of double toe loops, and a clean, graceful program. Today such a simple performance, however pleasing to watch, wouldn't win a hometown skating championship. Nowadays you must do at least three triple jumps, several combination jumps, a host of spins, and lots of fancy footwork. On top of that, your program must have *style,* or the scores for artistic impression will look more like grade point averages than the 5.8s and 5.9s you need to win the gold.

At one point in the TV coverage, the commentator mentioned that Katarina Witt planned to skate the same program with which she had won the gold medal six years earlier at the Calgary Olympics. He added that it was unlikely Ms. Witt would place near the top even if she gave a clean performance—the very best programs only six years ago simply weren't demanding enough for competition today.

Think about that. Are skaters today actually better than the skaters of a quarter century ago? Of course, but not because *Homo sapiens* has evolved to a higher state of athletic capability. Some of the improvements in today's performances, I'm sure, are a result of better skates and ice arenas. But the dominant reason for the improvement is that each year skaters raise their standards as they try to dethrone the latest national or world champion. Skaters 25 years ago could have included all those triple and combination jumps in their routines, but they didn't need to, so they didn't stretch themselves to master those feats.

In the book *Peopleware*, Tom DeMarco and Timothy Lister describe a similar difference in standards of performance among programmers who work for different companies. DeMarco and Lister conducted "coding wars" in which they gave a programming task to two programmers from every company participating in one of the contests. They found that the results differed remarkably from one programmer to the next, at times by as much as 11 to 1 in performance. That disparity is probably not too surprising. The surprising news is that programmers from the same company tended to produce similar results. If one did poorly, so would the other. Likewise, if one did well, both did well, even though the two programmers were working independently. DeMarco and Lister point out that the work environments at the companies could account for some of the difference in performance among the companies, but I believe the major reason for the 11 to 1 variance is that the acceptable skill level for the "average programmer" varies from one company to the next.

When was the last time you heard a lead say to a programmer, "I'm disappointed in you. You're doing just what you're expected to do"? Whether a company is aware of the phenomenon or not, its programmers have an average skill level, and once a programmer reaches that average level, the pressure to continue learning eases up even though the programmer might still be capable of dramatic improvement. The programmers are like those ice skaters 25 years ago—good enough. And leads tend not to spend time training people who are already doing their job at an acceptable level. They work with people who haven't yet reached that level.

Having a team of programmers who do what is expected is not good enough. An effective lead perpetually raises the standards, as coaches for Olympic-class skaters must do. As you raise the programming standards of your team, you'll ultimately raise the standards—the average—of your whole company.

FIVE-YEAR TENDERFEET

Occasionally I'll run across a programmer who after five or more years still works on the same project he or she was first assigned to. No problem with that, but in many cases I find that the programmer is not only on the same project but also doing the same job. If the programmer was assigned to the Microsoft Excel project to work on Macintosh-specific features, for instance, that's what he'll still be doing—as the specialist in that area. If the programmer was assigned to the compiler's code optimizer project, years later she'll still be working on that isolated chunk of code—again, as the specialist.

From a project standpoint, creating long-term specialists for specific parts of your product is a good idea, but creating specialists can backfire if you don't educate them wisely. You'll cripple those programmers and ultimately hurt your project and your company if you don't see to it that your specialists continue to learn new skills.

Suppose that Wilbur, a newly hired programmer, spends his first year becoming your file converter specialist and then spends the next four years writing filters to read and write the file formats of competing products. There's no question that such work is important, but Wilbur will have gained a year's worth of real experience and then tapered off, learning little else for the next four years. Wilbur would claim that he has five years of programming experience, but that would be misleading—he would in fact have one year's experience five times over.

If Wilbur had spent the last four of those five years working on other areas of the application, he'd have a much wider range of skills. If he had been moved around to work on different aspects of a mainstream

Windows or Macintosh application, for instance, he would have had an opportunity to develop all of this additional know-how:

◆ How to create and manipulate the user interface libraries— the menu manager, the dialog manager, the window manager—and all of the user interface gadgets you'd create with those libraries.

◆ How to hook into the help library to provide context-sensitive help for any new dialogs or other user interface extensions he incorporates into the application.

◆ How to use the graphics library to draw shapes, plot bit maps, do off-screen drawing, handle color palettes, and so on, for display devices with various characteristics.

◆ How to send output to printers, achieving the highest quality for each device, and how to make use of special features unique to each device, such as the ability of PostScript printers to print watermarks and hairlines.

◆ How to handle international issues such as double-byte characters, country-specific time and date formats, text orientation, and so on.

◆ How to handle the issues related to running an application in a networked environment.

◆ How to share data with other applications, whether the task is as simple as putting the data on the system clipboard or as complex as using the Windows Dynamic Data Exchange library or the Object Linking and Embedding library.

◆ How to write code that will work on all the popular microcomputer operating systems—MS-DOS, Windows, Windows NT, OS/2, and the Macintosh.

◆ . . .

You get the idea. These skills are easily within the grasp of any programmer who works on a Windows or Macintosh application for five years—provided that every new task contains an as-yet-unlearned element that forces a programmer to learn and grow.

Compare the two skill sets. If you were to start a new team, which Wilbur would you want more, the five-year file converter specialist or the Wilbur with one year's experience in writing file converters plus four more years' experience with the varied skills in the list? Remember, both Wilburs have worked for five years. . .

A lead's natural tendency when assigning tasks would be to give all the file converter work to Wilbur because he's the specialist in that area. It's not until the Wilburs of the world threaten to leave their projects for more interesting work that leads switch mental gears and start throwing new and different tasks their way.

But "if the specialists aren't doing the tasks they're expert in, wouldn't they be working more slowly on tasks they know less about?" Or to put it another way, "Don't you lose time by not putting the most experienced programmer on each task?"

If you view the project in terms of its specific tasks, the answer must be Yes, each task is being done more slowly than it could be done by a specialist. However, that little setback is more than compensated for when you look at the project as a whole. If you're constantly training team members so that they're proficient in all areas of your project, you build a much stronger team, one in which most team members can handle any unexpected problem. If a killer bug shows up, you don't need to rely on your specialist to fix it—anybody can fix it. If you need to implement a new feature in an existing body of code, any of many team members can efficiently do the work, not just one. Team members also know more about common subsystems, so you reduce duplicate code and improve product-wide design. The entire team has versatile skill sets.

Your team may be losing little bits of time during development as they learn new skills and gain experience, but for each minute they lose learning a new skill, they save multiple minutes in the future as they use that skill again and again. Constant training is an investment, one that offers tremendous leverage and tremendous rewards.

———◆———

Don't allow programmers to stagnate.
Constantly expose each team member
to new areas of the project.

———◆———

REUSABLE SKILLS

At Microsoft, when a novice programmer moves onto a project, he or she is typically given introductory work such as tracking down bugs and incorporating small changes here and there. Then gradually, as the programmer learns more about the program, the tasks become increasingly more difficult, until the programmer is implementing full-blown megafeatures. This gradualist approach makes sense because you can't very well have novices making major changes to code they know nothing about. My only disagreement with this approach is that the tasks are assigned according to their difficulty rather than according to the breadth of skills they could teach the programmer. As you assign tasks to programmers, keep the skills-teaching idea in mind. Don't assign successive tasks solely on the basis of difficulty; make sure that each task will teach a new skill as well, even if that means moving a novice programmer more quickly to difficult features. Even better, assign tasks at first that teach skills of benefit not only to your project but to the whole company.

In a spreadsheet program, for instance, tasks might range from implementing a new dialog of some sort to working on the recalculation engine. The skills a programmer would learn from these two tasks fall at two extremes: one skill has nothing to do with spreadsheets specifically, and the other historically has little use outside spreadsheet programming. Putting a programmer on the recalculation engine would be educational and would provide a valuable service to the project, but the skill wouldn't be as transferable as knowing how to implement a dialog would be. Learning how to create and manipulate dialogs could be useful in every project the company might undertake.

Creating a better "average programmer" means raising the standard throughout the company, not just on your project. You could assign programmers a random variety of tasks and ensure that team members would constantly learn, but you can do better than that. Analyze each task from the standpoint of the skills it calls upon, and assign it to the programmer who most needs to learn those skills. An experienced programmer should already know how to create dialogs, manipulate windows, change font sizes, and so on. She is ready to develop less globally useful—more specialized—skills such as the ability to add new macro functions to the spreadsheet's macro language. At some point, she'll know the program so well that in order to continue learning she'll have to move to extremely project-specific work such as implementing an even smarter recalculation engine.

A novice team member should be assigned a few tasks in which he must learn to create dialogs, followed by a few tasks that force him to manipulate windows, and so on. Deliberately assign tasks that cumulatively require all the general skills. That way, if the division should be reorganized and the programmer should find himself on another project, the skills he's learned will still be useful.

This is another example of a small system that produces greater results. Which specific work you assign to a novice programmer may not make much difference in the progress of your own project, but by first exposing a new programmer to a wide range of general skills that he or she can bring to any project, you make the programmer more valuable to the company.

---◆---

When training programmers, focus first on skills that are useful to the entire company and second on skills specific to your project.

---◆---

GIVE EXPERTS THE BOOT

If you constantly expose a team member to new tasks that call for new skills, he or she will eventually reach a point at which your project no longer offers room to grow. You could let the programmer's growth stall while your project benefited from his or her expertise, but for the benefit of the company, you should kick such an expert off your team. If you allow programmers to stagnate, you hurt the overall skill level of the company. You have a duty to the programmers and to the company to find the programmers positions in which they can grow.

Am I joking? No.

The tendency is to jealously hold onto the team's best programmers even if they aren't learning anything new. Why would you want to kick your best programmer off the team? That would be insane. . .

113

In Chapter 3, I talked about a dialog manager library that the Word for Windows group had been complaining about. Although I wasn't the lead of the dialog manager team then, I did eventually wind up in that position. And there came a point at which the main programmer on the team had reached a plateau: he wasn't learning anything new within the constraints of that project. Besides, he was tired of working on the same old code. He needed to stretch his skills.

When I asked whether he knew of any interesting openings on other projects, he described a position in Microsoft's new user interface lab in which he would be able to design and implement experimental user interface ideas. In many ways, it seemed like a dream job for the programmer, so I talked to the lab's director to verify that the job was a good opportunity for this programmer to learn new skills. The position looked great. In less than a week, the dialog team's best programmer was gone, leaving a gaping hole.

In these situations, you can either panic or get excited. I get excited because I believe that gaping holes attract team members who are ready to grow and fill them. Somebody always rises to the occasion, experiencing tremendous growth as he or she fills the gap. The dialog team's gap proved to be no different. Another member jumped headlong into the opening.

Occasionally I'd bump into the lab director and ask how the project was going. "Beyond my wildest dreams," he'd say. "We're accomplishing more than I ever imagined or hoped for." He had been expecting to get an entry-level programmer, but he'd gotten a far more experienced programmer, and his group was barreling along.

The dialog manager group with its new lead programmer was barreling along too. The new lead had just needed the room to grow, room that had been taken up by the expert programmer.

You might think that kicking your best programmer off the team would do irreparable harm to your project. It rarely works out that way. In this case, the dialog team experienced a short-term loss, but the company saw a huge long-term gain. Instead of a slow-moving user interface project and two programmers who had stopped growing, the company got a fast-moving user interface project and two programmers who were undergoing rapid growth. That outcome shouldn't be too surprising. As long as its people are growing, so is the company.

*Don't jealously hold onto your best program-
mers if they've stopped growing. For the good
of the programmers, their replacements, and
the company, transfer stalled programmers to
new projects where growth can continue.*

The Cross-Pollination Theory—Dismissed

Occasionally I'll run across the idea that companies should periodically shuffle programmers around so that they can transfer ideas from one project to another. It's the cross-pollination theory.

The cross-pollination theory appeals to me because its purpose is to improve development processes within the company, but in my experience the cross-pollination practice falls short of its goal, and for a simple reason: it ignores human nature. Advocates of the theory assume that programmers who move to brand-new groups will teach the new groups the special knowledge they bring with them. But how many people feel comfortable doing that in a new environment? And even if a programmer would feel comfortable as an evangelist, how many groups would appreciate some newcomer's telling them what they should do? A new lead might feel fine propounding fresh ideas hours or days into the project, but nonleads? It might be years, if ever, before a programmer would feel comfortable enough to push his or her ideas beyond a narrow work focus.

Advocates of the cross-pollination theory assume that new people bring new knowledge into the group. In fact, that's backwards from what actually happens: new people don't bring their knowledge into the new group as much as they get knowledge from the new group. New people find themselves immersed in different, and possibly better, ways of doing things. And they learn. The primary benefit is to the person doing the moving. If that person can continue to grow on his or her current project, why cause disruption? Let the people who are stagnating move to other teams and learn more. Don't shuffle people around to other teams expecting them to spread the word. They usually won't.

The New Year's Syndrome

Not all skills can be attained in the course of doing well-chosen project tasks. A skill such as learning to lead projects must be deliberately pursued as a goal in itself. The person must decide to be a good lead and then take steps to make it happen. It's proactive learning, as opposed to learning as a side effect of working on a task.

If you want your team members to make great leaps as well as take incremental daily steps to improvement, you must see that they actively pursue the greater goals.

The traditional approach to establishing such goals is to list them as personal skill objectives on the annual performance review. We all know what happens to those goals: except for a few self-motivated and driven individuals, people forget them before the week is over. Then along comes the next review, and their leads are dismayed to see that none of the personal growth goals have been fulfilled. I think we've all seen this happen—it's the New Year's Resolution Syndrome, only the date is different.

Such goals fall by the wayside because there are no attack plans for achieving them or because, if there are such plans, the plans have no teeth—just as those postmortem plans I spoke of in Chapter 4 had no teeth. Listing a goal on a review form with no provision for how it will be achieved is like saying "I'm going to be rich" but never deciding exactly how you're going to make that happen. To achieve the goal, you need a concrete plan, a realistic deadline, and a constant focus on the goal.

One way to ensure that each team member makes a handful of growth leaps each year is to align the personal growth goals with the two-month project milestones. One goal per milestone. That practice enables team members to make six leaps a year—more if there are multiple goals per milestone.

Improvement goals don't need to be all-encompassing. They can be as simple as reading one good technical or business book each milestone or developing a good habit such as stepping through all new code in the debugger to proactively look for bugs. Sometimes the growth goal can be to correct a bad work habit such as writing code on the fly at the keyboard—the design-as-you-go approach to programming.

Read Any Good Books Lately?

I read constantly to gain new knowledge and insights. Why spend years of learning by trial and error when I can pick up a good book and in a few days achieve insights that took someone else decades to formulate? What a deal. If team members read just six insightful books a year, imagine how that could influence their work. I particularly like books that transform insights into strategies you can immediately carry out. That's why I wrote both *Writing Solid Code* and this book as strategy books. But mine are hardly the first. *The Elements of Programming Style*, by Brian Kernighan and P. J. Plauger, was first published in 1974 and is still valuable today. *Writing Efficient Programs*, by Jon Bentley, is another excellent strategy book, as is Andrew Koenig's *C Traps & Pitfalls* for C and C++ programmers.

In addition to these strategy books, there are dozens of other excellent—and practical—books on software development, from Gerald Weinberg's classic *The Psychology of Computer Programming* to the much more recent *Code Complete*, by Steve McConnell, which includes a full chapter on "Where to Go for More Information," with brief descriptions of dozens of the industry's best books, articles, and organizations.

But don't limit yourself to books and articles that talk strictly about software development. Mark McCormack's *What They Don't Teach You at Harvard Business School*, for instance, may focus on project management at IMG, his sports marketing firm, and Michael Gerber's *The E-Myth* may focus on how to build franchise operations, but books like these provide a wealth of information you can apply immediately to software development. And don't make the mistake of thinking that such books are suitable only for project leads. The greenest member of the team can benefit from such books.

To ensure their personal interest in achieving such goals, I encourage team members to choose the skills they want to pursue, and I merely verify that each goal is worth going after:

◆ The skill or knowledge would benefit the programmer, the project, and the company. Learning LISP could be useful to an individual, but for a company such as Microsoft, it would be as useful as scuba gear to a swordfish.

◆ The goal is achievable within a reasonable time frame such as the two-month milestone interval. Anybody can read a good technical book in two months. It's much harder to become a C++ expert in that short a time.

◆ The goal has measurable results. A goal such as "becoming a better programmer" is hard to measure, whereas a goal such as "developing the habit of stepping through all new code in the debugger to catch bugs" is easy to measure: the programmer either has or hasn't developed the habit.

◆ Ideally, the skill or knowledge will have immediate usefulness to the project. A programmer might acquire a worthwhile skill, but if he has no immediate use for the new skill, he's likely to lose or forget what he's learned.

Such a list keeps the focus on skills that are useful to the individual, to his or her project, and to the company—in sum, it focuses on the kinds of skills a programmer needs in order to be considered for promotion. If the programmer can't think of a skill to focus on, choose one yourself: "What additional skills would this programmer need for me to feel comfortable about promoting him or her?"

———◆———

Make sure each team member learns
one new significant skill at least
every two months.

———◆———

Train Your Replacement

Programmers don't usually choose to pursue management skills unless they have reason to believe they're going to need those skills. Find the people who have an interest in becoming team leads, and help them acquire the skills they'll need to lead teams in the future. And remember, unless you plan to lead your current team forever, you need to train somebody to replace you. If you don't, you might find yourself in a tough spot, wanting to lead an exciting new project and unable to make the move because nobody is capable of taking over your current job.

IN THE MOMENT

A particularly good approach to identifying skills for your team members to develop is to set a growth goal the moment you see a problem or an opportunity. When I spot programmers debugging ineffectively, I show them a better way and get them to commit to mastering the new practice over the next few weeks. When a programmer remarks that she wants to learn techniques for writing fast code, I hand her a copy of Jon Bentley's *Writing Efficient Programs* and secure her commitment to reading it—and later discussing it. If I turn up an error-prone coding practice as I review some new code, I stop and describe my concern to the programmer and get him to commit to weeding the practice out of his programming style.

I'm big on setting improvement goals in the moment. Such goals have impact because they contain a strong emotional element. Which do you think would influence a programmer more: showing him code he wrote a year ago and asking him to weed out a risky coding practice or showing him a piece of code he wrote yesterday and asking him to weed out the practice?

I once trained a lead who would search me out every time he had a problem. He'd say, "The WordSmasher group doesn't have time to implement their Anagram feature, and they want to know if we can help out. What should we do?" The lead came to me so often that I eventually concluded he wasn't doing his own thinking. When I explained my feelings to him, he replied that he always thought through the possible solutions but didn't want to make a mistake. That was why he was asking me what to do. I pointed out that his approach made him seem too dependent and that we needed to work on the problem.

I understood the lead's need for confirmation, so I told him to feel free to talk to me about problems as they arose, on one condition: instead of dumping the problem in my lap, he was to

◆ Explain the problem to me.

◆ Describe any solutions he could come up with, including the pros and cons of each one.

◆ Suggest a course of action and tell me why he chose that course.

Once the lead began following this practice, my perception of him changed immediately and radically. On 9 out of 10 occasions, all I had to do was say, "Yes! Do it." to a fully considered plan of action. The few times I thought a different course of action made sense, I explained my rationale to him, we talked it over, and he got new insights. Sometimes I got the new insights. We'd go with his original suggestion if my solution was merely different and not demonstrably better.

This improvement took almost no new effort on either his part or mine, but the shift in his effectiveness was dramatic. We went from a relationship in which I felt as if I were making all his decisions to one in which I was acknowledging his own good decisions. My attitude changed from "this guy is too dependent and doesn't think things through" to "this guy is thoughtful and makes good decisions." His attitude changed too, from being afraid to make decisions to knowing that most of his decisions were solid. It didn't take too many weeks for our "What should I do?" meetings to all but disappear. He consulted me only for truly puzzling problems for which he couldn't come up with any good solution.

What caused this dramatic change? Was it a major revamping of this person's skills? No, it was a simple change in communication style provoked by my realization that he had become too dependent. A minor change, a major improvement.

———◆———

Take immediate corrective action
the moment you realize that an
area needs improvement.

———◆———

AFTER-THE-FACT MANAGEMENT

Note that I gave that lead on-the-spot feedback and a goal he could act on immediately. I didn't wait for the annual review. I don't believe the annual review is a good tool for planning personal improvement or achievement goals. In my experience such a delayed response to problems isn't effective—at least not unless the annual review also contains detailed attack plans for the goals. Another problem with using the annual review for improvement goals is that few leads are able to effectively evaluate anyone's growth over such a long period of time.

We've all heard stories about the review in which the manager brings up a problem with the programmer's performance that has never been mentioned before to justify giving the programmer a review rating lower than the programmer expected. In shock, the programmer stammers, "Can you give me an example of what you're talking about?" The manager stumbles a bit and comes up with something, that, yes, the programmer did do, or failed to do, but which sounds absurdly out of proportion in the context of the programmer's performance for the whole review period. "You've given me a low rating because of that?" Of course, it sounds ridiculous to the manager too, so she scrambles to come up with another example of the problem but usually can't because so much time has passed.

Then, of course, once the programmer leaves the meeting and has time to think about the review a bit, his or her reaction is anger. "Why didn't she *tell me* something was wrong, rather than waiting a year? How could I have fixed something I didn't even know was wrong?"

I've lost track of the number of times I've heard people say that about their managers.

What if professional football teams worked that way? What if coaches waited until the end of the season to tell players what they're doing wrong?

"Mad Dog, I'm putting you on the bench next season."

"Huh? What? I thought I played great," says Mad Dog, confused.

"You played well, but at each snap of the ball, you hesitated before running into position."

"I did?"

"Yes, you did, and that prevented you from catching as many passes as you could have. I'm putting you on the bench until something changes. Of course, this means that your yearly salary will drop from $5.2 million to $18,274. But don't worry, you'll still have your benefits—free soft drinks and hot dogs at the concession stand, and discounted souvenirs."

Mad Dog, particularly mad now: "If you spotted this, *why didn't you tell me earlier?* I could have *done* something about it."

"Hey, I'm telling you now, at our end-of-the-season contract review."

Sounds pretty silly, doesn't it? But how does it differ from the way many leads make use of the annual review?

Remember the lead I felt was too dependent and was not thinking things through? The common approach at most companies would be to wait until the end of the review period and note the problem on the review document:

```
Relies too much on other people to make his decisions;
doesn't take the time to think problems through.
```

Then, of course, after the confused exchange at the review meeting, the attack plan to fix the problem would be something like this:

```
I won't rely on other people to make my decisions for me;
I'll think my problems through.
```

That attack plan won't be effective because it is too vague. The plan doesn't describe what the person is to do, how he is to do it, or how to measure the results—the plan has no teeth. In all likelihood, the problem will still exist a year later, at the next review.

Personnel reviews, as I've seen them done, are almost totally worthless as a tool to promote employee growth. Don't bother with the new goals part of the review. Actively promote improvement by seizing the moment and aligning growth goals with your project milestones. Use the formal review to *document* employee growth during the review period—that's what upper management really needs to see anyway. Listing areas in which people could improve doesn't really tell upper management much. Documenting the important skills that people have actually mastered and how they applied those skills demonstrates constant growth and gives upper management something tangible with which to justify raises, bonuses, and promotions.

———◆———

*Don't use the annual personnel review to set
achievement goals. Use the review to document
the personal growth goals achieved during
the review period.*

———◆———

THOROUGHLY KNOWLEDGEABLE

Most of the interviews I conducted at Microsoft were with college students about to graduate, but occasionally I interviewed a working programmer who wanted to join Microsoft. At first I was surprised to find that the experienced programmers who came from small, upstart companies seemed, in general, more skilled than the experienced programmers from the big-name software houses, even though the programmers had been working for comparable numbers of years. I believe that what I've been talking about in this chapter accounts for the difference. The programmers working for the upstart companies had to be knowledgeable in dozens of areas, not expert in one. Their companies didn't have the luxury of staffing 30-person teams in which each individual could focus on one primary area. Out of necessity, those programmers were forced to learn more skills.

As a lead—even in a big outfit that can afford specialists—you must create the pressure to learn new skills. It doesn't matter whether you teach team members personally or whether they get their training through books and technical seminars. As long as your teams continue to experience constant, unceasing improvement, the "average programmer" in your company will continue to get better—like those Olympic-class skaters—and that can only be good for your project, for your company, and ultimately for your customers.

HIGHLIGHTS

◆   Never allow a team member to stagnate by limiting him or her to work on one specific part of your project. Once programmers have mastered an area, move them to a new area where they can continue to improve their skills.

◆   Skills vary in usefulness from those that can be applied to any project to those that can be applied to only one specific type of project. When you train your team members, maximize their value to the company by first training them in the most widely useful skills and save the project-specific skills for last.

◆ It's tempting to hold onto your top programmers, but if they aren't learning anything new on your project, you're stalling their growth and holding the company's average skill level down. When a top programmer leaves the team for a new position, not only does he or she start growing again, but so does his or her replacement. A double benefit.

◆ To ensure that the skills of the team members are expanding on a regular basis, see that every team member is always working on at least one major improvement goal. The easiest approach is to align growth goals with the two-month milestones, enabling at least six skill leaps a year—which is six more per year than many programmers currently experience. If Wilbur, the file converter specialist, had read just 6 high-quality technical books a year, after his first five years of programming he'd have read 30 such books. How do you suppose that would have influenced his work? Or what if Wilbur had mixed the reading of 15 good books with the mastery of 15 valuable skills over that first five years?

◆ The best growth goals emerge from a strong, immediate need. If you find a team member working inefficiently or repeating the same type of mistake, seize the opportunity to create a specific improvement goal that the team member can act on immediately. Because such on-the-spot goals lend themselves to immediate action for a definite purpose, the programmer is likely to give them more attention than he would give to abstract goals devised for an annual review.

7

IT'S ALL ABOUT ATTITUDE

In Chapter 6, I emphasized how important it is that you work with team members to improve their skills and knowledge. Exposing team members to new kinds of tasks promotes incremental learning, and getting the programmers to read books and develop new coding habits makes for even more impressive results. But the most profound improvements come about when a team adopts new attitudes about how to develop products.

BUGGY ATTITUDES

As I said in Chapter 1, the job of the professional programmer is to write useful, bug-free code in a reasonable time frame. A key point in that idea is that the code be "bug-free." Unfortunately, writing bug-free code is hard. If it weren't, everybody would write bug-free code.

.One pervasive attitude in programming shops is that bugs are inevitable and there's not much you can do about them except to fix them when they show up. While common, that attitude is completely wrongheaded. Programmers can make great strides toward writing bug-free code, but it requires extra effort, effort that programmers won't willingly make until they internalize the attitude that writing bug-free code is critical to product development.

One simple—and obvious—technique I use to catch an entire class of bugs is to turn on the compiler's optional warnings, the ones that display an error message for correct, yet probably buggy, code. For example, many C compilers have an optional warning to catch this common mistake:

```
if (ch = tab_char)          /* Note single = sign. */
    ...
```

The code above is perfectly correct C code, yet it contains a bug that the compiler can detect. The tab character is being assigned to *ch* when what the programmer intended was to *compare* the tab character to *ch*:

```
if (ch == tab_char)         /* Note double = sign. */
    ...
```

Enabling just one commonly supported compiler warning would allow the compiler to flag all such erroneous assignment bugs, yet I've worked with many programmers who absolutely refuse to use that option. The programmers feel that the warning interferes with writing code because the compiler gives them a warning even when they intentionally make an assignment in an *if* statement, forcing them to rewrite their code. Instead of writing

```
if (ch = readkeyboard())
    process character typed by the user
```

which would generate a warning, they would have to make a slight change, having to write either

```
ch = readkeyboard();
if (ch != nul_char)
    process character typed by the user
```

or the more terse

```
if ((ch = readkeyboard()) != nul_char)
    process character typed by the user
```

Neither of the two work-arounds would generate any additional object code because both simply make the test against the nul character explicit instead of implicit. And to most C programmers, either of the work-arounds is as clear as the original code—possibly more so if a programmer is reading the code quickly.

But some programmers are adamant. They refuse to use optional compiler warnings. "I should be able to write code any way I want," they say. "The compiler should never issue a warning for perfectly legal code." Given the intensity with which some programmers talk about this issue, you'd think I was suggesting that they give up their desktop PCs and go back to using punch cards.

This issue points up a difference in programmer attitudes toward bugs. Since I habitually use the compiler work-arounds, I never get warnings unless I've actually created a bug by mistake—and I want to know when I've made such a mistake. To me, being able to find bugs easily is far more important than what I view as an inconsequential style change. Programmers who refuse to enable any compiler warnings, it seems to me, are more concerned with personal expression than with detecting bugs. If those programmers aren't willing to make such minor changes, what are the odds of their making more critical changes? Would they adopt the team-wide or company-wide naming or coding style? Would they agree to give up favorite but error-prone coding tricks? Would they even entertain the idea of stepping through all their new code in a debugger to detect implementation bugs at the earliest possible moment?

Yes, writing bug-free code takes effort, effort that programmers won't make unless their attitude is that bugs are simply unacceptable.

On my own projects, I review every reported bug, keeping an eye out for bugs that should have been caught by someone's using the project's unit tests or stepping through the code with the debugger. Any programmer who allows such bugs to get into the master sources needs more training—he or she is failing to meet the quality bar.

Novice programmers tend to give up far too early because they have the basic attitude that their code probably *doesn't* contain bugs:

I'm done because the code compiles without error and appears to run correctly.

Novice programmers have that attitude because they haven't yet been caught over and over again by overflow and underflow bugs, signed and unsigned data type bugs, general type conversion bugs, precedence bugs, subtle logic bugs, and all the other bugs that go unnoticed when novices read code in the editor and that show up only for special cases when they run their code—cases they haven't yet learned to test for.

Fix Bugs Early

The primary reason I push hard for programmers to step through their code the moment they write it and to run their unit tests is that it takes so much less time than letting even a single bug slip by and find its way into the product's master sources.

The moment a bug makes it into the master sources, it not only hurts the product but costs everyone huge amounts of time. The programmer on her end has to stop working on features and track down the bug, apply a fix, test the change (we hope), and report the bug as fixed. Back to Testing. Since a bug was found, the testers must retest the entire feature to ensure that the fix works and that the fix hasn't broken anything else. Then they must write a regression test for the bug. If the regression test can't be automated, a tester must manually verify that the bug has not returned in every future testing release.

Compare all that effort expended on a single bug to the effort it would take for the programmer to step through the code and run the unit test before ever merging the feature into the master sources. If the programmer finds the bug before sending the feature to Testing, none of that protracted effort I just outlined is necessary. That's why I say that it's so much cheaper for programmers to find their bugs before the testing team ever sees the code.

Experienced programmers who consistently have low bug rates have learned that they're more likely to find Bigfoot slurping ice cream at the local Baskin-Robbins than they are to write bug-free code. Unlike the novices, such experienced programmers assume that their code probably *does* contain bugs:

Until I find all the unknown bugs in this code, I'm not done.

It might seem that with such an attitude, programmers could go overboard in testing their code, but I've yet to see that happen. Anybody who is smart enough to write programs realizes when he or she is wasting time on redundant tests. Somebody smart enough to write programs doesn't always realize, though, when he or she isn't testing thoroughly enough. It's hard to know that you've forgotten to test a unique scenario or two.

———◆———

Be sure programmers understand that writing bug-free code is so difficult that they can't afford not to use every means to detect and prevent bugs.

———◆———

RESISTING EFFORT

One question I regularly ask as I review both designs and implementations is "How error-prone is this design or implementation?" I look for weaknesses and try to judge how risky the code would be to modify. When I find a weakness, I take steps to overcome it, by either changing the design to get rid of the weakness or introducing debug code into the program to monitor the implementation for trouble.

I once reviewed a new feature that had been implemented using a large table of numbers. I like table-driven implementations, as a rule, because they're usually concise and less prone to errors, but they do have a weakness in that the data in the table could be wrong. I pointed this weakness out to the programmer who had implemented the code for the feature and asked him to add some debug code to validate the table during program initialization. Without thinking, the programmer blurted, "Writing that code will take too much time!"

Klaxons blared. Red lights flashed. Flares went skyward.

Those alarms went off because that programmer committed what I consider to be a fundamental error in intelligent decision making: He didn't ask himself whether my request made sense. Instead, he pounced on how much extra time he thought writing the debug code would take.

That programmer's first response should have been "Does the request make sense?" His second response should have been "Does it fulfill the project goals and coding priorities?" The question whether the task would take too much time or effort should have come third in the order of evaluation.

After the programmer had calmed down, I explained my objections to his decision-making strategy and asked him to start evaluating requests according to the order of questions I've described:

◆ Does adding the debug code make sense?

◆ If so, does adding the debug code fulfill the goals and coding priorities of the project?

◆ Finally, is adding the debug code important enough to justify the time that will have to be spent doing it?

After we stepped through this evaluation process, the programmer— still reluctant—agreed to implement the debug code.

Thirty minutes later he came into my office, having added the debug code to the program, and showed me three potential problems in the table that the debug code had flagged. Two of the problems were obvious bugs—once they had been pointed out. The third problem was confusing: neither he nor I could see the bug the debug code was reporting. We thought at first that the debug code itself might have a bug, causing an invalid report. But if the debug code was buggy, that bug wasn't obvious to us either. We pondered the suspected bug for nearly 10 minutes before we finally realized that the data in the table was indeed wrong. That bug was hard to spot even though the debug code pointed right at the erroneous table entry. Imagine how hard the bug would have been to spot without the debug code to lead us to it.

That programmer learned two valuable lessons that day. First, that it's still worthwhile to add debug support to code you already think is bug-free. And second, that the first reaction to any proposal should never be "That will take too much time" or its disguised sibling, "That's too hard (and would therefore require too much time)."

———◆———

Watch out for and correct the "it's too much work" reaction. Train programmers to first consider whether the task makes sense and whether it matches up with the project goals and priorities.

———◆———

CAN'TTITUDE

I've worked with many programmers—and project leads—who hardly ever hit upon new ideas or employ new development strategies because they shut down their thought processes before they ever get started. Have you ever been at a meeting in which some poor soul proposed a new idea only to be bludgeoned by the others with all the reasons the idea couldn't possibly work, with how impossible it would be to get upper management to agree, or simply with the bald "You can't do that! It's never been done before!"

This "can't attitude"—can'ttitude—is so destructive to creativity and problem solving that I try to discourage it whenever I run across it. I have a rule—and in this case it *is* a rule—that nobody on my teams is allowed to say that something can't be done. They can say it would be "hard" or that it would "take tons of time," but they can't say "can't." My reason:

> *When somebody says that something can't be done, he or she is usually wrong.*

I learned long ago to disregard most claims that you can't do such and such. More often than not, the person who says that hasn't given one iota of thought—at least not lately—to whether you really can't. Yes, of course, you can come up with hundreds of hypothetical, and absurd, situations in which something can't be done—getting all 2704 known bugs fixed by noon tomorrow, for instance. But usually when people make suggestions that get shot down with *can'ts*, the suggestions aren't absurd; if they were, the people wouldn't have proposed them.

Whenever you hear somebody say that something can't be done, ask yourself whether that person seems to have given any real thought to the question. If you know the person has, consider whether his or her evaluation is dated. Things change, especially in our industry. Maybe what couldn't have been accomplished last year can be accomplished fairly handily now—particularly if the proposal revolves around a size or speed trade-off. There was a time, after all, when people maintained, "You can't do a graphical user interface. It would take tons of memory and be unbearably slow." That was once true. Now it's not.

Sometimes it's a political or administrative matter that meets with the *can't* resistance. Microsoft leads will tell you that you can't give back-to-back promotions or a raise bigger than the biggest allowed, but I've done both of those things in exceptional circumstances. Was it easy? Definitely not. I had to go out of my way to prove that what I was asking for was in the best interest of the company. I was successful because what I asked for made sense, despite corporate policy. Those accomplishments weren't impossible to achieve, just hard.

Many times people latch onto the "can't be done" attitude simply because whatever you're talking about is outside their experience.

In 1988, when we were nearing completion of Microsoft Excel 1.5 for the Macintosh, upper management was already talking about the 2.0 release. The plan was that the Macintosh team would continue to port features from the Windows version of Excel, implementing look-alike features when the Windows Excel code couldn't merely be swiped and reworked to fit. Having spent two years doing just such work, I wasn't thrilled with the idea. I felt there were too many problems with that approach. Despite their external similarities, there were numerous differences between Excel for Windows and Excel for the Macintosh because they were, in fact, two different bodies of code. I also felt that Excel for the Macintosh would never be on a par with its Windows sibling. The Windows product was already considerably more powerful than the Macintosh product, and their team was larger than ours—a recipe for ever-widening feature disparity and incompatibility.

There was also a serious problem with the Macintosh implementation. Because of a design decision that had a pervasive influence on the code, the Macintosh application couldn't use more than 1 MB of RAM. Even worse, the code had to reside in the *first* 1 MB of RAM. Users were complaining loudly—why couldn't Excel use the other 7 MB of RAM in their systems? Outrageous!

Programmers at Apple Computer discovered Excel's predilection for low memory addresses as they were developing MultiFinder, their then-new multitasking operating system. The Apple programmers had designed MultiFinder to load applications from the top of memory down, but they discovered that Excel wouldn't work unless it was loaded at the very bottom of memory. Around their shop, Excel became known as "the application afraid of heights." To get Excel and MultiFinder to work together, Apple's programmers included special code in MultiFinder to look for and accommodate Excel, uniquely loading it into low memory. And they asked Microsoft to work on Excel's acrophobia, a phobia that had already been "cured" in the Windows version of the product. In fact, the Windows Excel team had done a line-by-line rewrite of the product and fixed numerous problems, with the result that their code far surpassed the Macintosh code in quality and maintainability.

When I looked at the 2.0 development plan to rip out Macintosh Excel's guts to fix the 1-MB problem and to port as many Windows Excel features as possible, I saw that the Macintosh team members would be spending all their time duplicating work that the Windows team had long ago completed. And we'd still end up with a somewhat incompatible and far less powerful product than theirs. That seemed like a big waste of time to me.

Why not instead, I thought, expend half as much energy to create a multi-platform version of Excel from the existing Windows sources? I'd spent years writing multi-platform code before joining Microsoft, so I knew what the challenges were in writing such code, and I couldn't see any reason why the Windows Excel code couldn't be modified to support the Macintosh. If we took that approach, I reasoned, the Macintosh product—being built from the same code—would be just as powerful as the Windows product and fully compatible. The 1-MB memory restriction would disappear, and instead of having to invest in the full development effort that would otherwise be required, Microsoft would be able to create future Macintosh releases at a fraction of the previous development cost.

When I talked to upper management about scrapping the 2.0 development plan in favor of creating a multi-platform version of Excel, they asked me to take a week to review the Excel for Windows sources and write an attack plan proposal for the work.

A week later, after I had released the attack plan to upper management and both Excel teams, I was taken aback by all the objections to what I proposed. Even though the attack plan was straightforward, people focused on all the problems they felt couldn't be overcome. I was surrounded by can'ttitude.

"Maguire is dreaming," said one programmer. "Windows and the Macintosh are just too different," said another. A third said, "Assuming we could create a multi-platform product, it would ruin Excel. The code would be too slow and too fat and wouldn't take advantage of the unique features of each platform." Still another said, "We don't have the time now. We should wait until after the next release"—as if there would be time *then*. One person even threatened to quit the company if we chose to take on the amount of work he thought it would take.

I had been expecting the plan to be wholeheartedly embraced. I got an education that day. I learned that fear of the unknown can affect even the best and most self-assured development teams.

A few days later, the Excel teams met with upper management, there was a vote—the only vote I ever saw at Microsoft—and the plan was shot down. There would be no multi-platform product, and work on Macintosh Excel 2.0 would go ahead as planned.

I was still reeling from the decision when we got word that Bill Gates, Microsoft's CEO, had read the proposed attack plan and thought that the multi-platform approach made sense. The work was on.

The team went on to do the multi-platform work in just eight months. And the application never fell prey to all those early concerns people had expressed. It's true that a few operations were a bit slower in the multi-platform version of Excel than in the original Macintosh version, but the slowdown was the result of lifting the 1-MB restriction, not of the multi-platform work. The product's speed would have been affected by the lifting of the restriction either way.

The Excel programmers were rightly proud of their accomplishment, and many went on to help other Microsoft project teams implement multi-platform code.

————◆————

Don't let can'ttitude discourage innovation.

————◆————

Don't Bring Me Problems! Bring Me Solutions!

The problem with can'ttitude—if there's enough of it—is that people stop speaking up when they see an opportunity for innovation, or worse, when they see a problem that needs to be fixed. Sadly, some project leads go out of their way to shut down people who would otherwise raise valid concerns. Have you ever been at a meeting in which somebody raised a problem and the lead barked back, "Don't bring up any problem you don't know how to solve—it wastes our time"?

Unfortunately, that approach leads team members to clam up until they can think of solutions for the problems they've noticed. A programmer could spot a serious problem affecting development but, not knowing how to solve the problem, might never bring it up for fear of getting a crushing and humiliating response.

Leads who insist that team members can't bring up any problems they don't know how to solve should instead realize that all problems need to be raised regardless of whether there is a known solution. Would you want a worker at a nuclear plant to clam up because she didn't know what to do about the green goo she found leaking from a critical part of the reactor? Of course not. She might not know how to handle the goo, but somebody else on the reactor team probably would know or would certainly be motivated to find a solution quickly.

Why should development teams be run any differently? Even if the person who brings up the problem doesn't have a solution, somebody else on the team might be able to come up with one. Problems that aren't brought up are problems that don't get solved.

It's Good Enough for Users

Occasionally I'll run into a programmer who thinks he or she is unique in requiring things from a product that mere users don't need.

One time I asked a programmer to demonstrate an important feature he had just completed. He launched the application and began showing me how the feature worked. The feature looked sharp, except that it seemed sluggish.

"Are you running the debug version of the code?" I asked, thinking that debug code must be responsible for the poky response.

"No, this is the ship version." He went on demonstrating.

"Have you thought about how to speed things up?"

"What do you mean?"

"I mean, don't you think the code is a bit slow?"

"Well, I wouldn't like it, but it'll be OK for the users."

I was shocked. "What makes you so different from the users? Especially in this case, when the users are other programmers *just like you?*"

I have never understood why some programmers think that users—whether they're other programmers or gourmet pasta shop owners—are any less concerned about speed and other aspects of quality than the programmer who wrote the code.

I'd argue that end users are *more* particular about speed and other aspects of quality since they actually use the features, whereas the programmers who write the code often don't. Do you think the programmers working on Microsoft's FORTRAN compiler use FORTRAN when they write code? Do the programmers who worked on Word's Mail Merge feature ever use that capability? What about Excel's macro language? Dozens of programmers have extended the macro language over the years, but how many have ever written their own user-defined macros? I'm not saying that all of these programmers are guilty of the gross disregard for the user expressed by that earlier programmer. That simply isn't so. My point is that programmers routinely implement code that they themselves never have occasion to use. Think about your own project. Do the programmers on your team actually use the code they write?

When programmers don't use the code they write, it's easy for them to distance themselves from the end user. This distancing may account for the occasional programmer who thinks that end users are bozos who aren't concerned about speed and other aspects of software quality—at least not to the same degree that the programmer himself would be.

To keep the end user in mind, programmers should measure their work against this reminder—you might want to put it on a large banner you hang over the entrance to your building:

> *The end user is at least as concerned about speed and other aspects*
> *of software quality as the programmer who implements the code.*

We all know that some users don't care much about the quality of the programs they use, as long as they aren't prevented from getting

---

Usability

When Microsoft first began conducting usability studies in the late 1980s to figure out how to make their products easier to use, their researchers found that 6 to 8 out of 10 users couldn't understand the user interface and get to most of the features. When they heard about those findings, the first question some programmers asked was "Where did we find eight dumb users?" They didn't consider the possibility that it might be the user interface that was dumb.

If the programmers on your team consciously or unconsciously believe that the users are unintelligent, you had better correct that attitude—and fast. Consider two teams, one on which the programmers believe that users are probably intelligent, discerning consumers and another on which the programmers assume that users are essentially dumb. Which team is more likely to take users' complaints seriously and act on them to improve the software? Which team is more likely to ask users for their opinions about new features that would improve the product? Which of the two teams is going to consistently put out a product that fits the users' needs? On the other hand, which team is more likely to ignore users' complaints and instead waste time on features that the users don't need or want? The basic attitude the team adopts toward the users can make a great difference in the quality of the product.

---

their jobs done. But if you want to ship great products, you can't target those unfussy people. You must target the users who do care whether a program is slow or quirky or contains bugs that can make it crash.

———◆———

Don't let programmers believe that
users don't care as much about software
quality as programmers do.

———◆———

BEWARE THE SUBSTANDARD FEATURE

I used to have the attitude that it was better to give the user a painfully slow feature, or an overly restrictive one, than to cut the feature and give the user nothing at all. "At least the user will have something between now and when we ship the more polished version in the next release," I'd reason. Eventually it dawned on me that users weren't aware of the choice I'd made—giving them something, even of substandard quality, over giving them nothing at all. Users, I realized, open the box, run the program, and see only that they've gotten another poorly implemented feature. "Why does it always take them two releases to get things right?" they wonder.

I've seen this reaction often enough now that rather than trying to give the user something, I cut any feature that doesn't meet the quality bar. Users rarely miss what they've never had, but if you give them a feature they feel is unpolished or frustrating to use, they're liable to think less of the whole program. If you give them several such features, they might start looking at your competitor's product.

It pains me to say this, but if a feature doesn't meet your quality bar, consider cutting it, even if it seems as if it could be a useful feature. Wait until the next release, and do it right. If the feature is so strategic that you feel you must ship it, it's also probably worth slipping your ship date to do it right.

———◆———

Don't ship substandard features.
Postpone them until you can implement
them properly.

———◆———

THE SENSITIVE PROGRAMMER

In Chapter 1, I described a situation in which a lead for a Windows-like user interface library had never bothered to view the library as one of the library's "customers" would. The lead had never considered the possibility that a library that wasn't backwards compatible would be frustrating to its users. I've seen this lack of appreciation for the users' perspective so many times that it's worth talking about.

When the Windows Excel team was rewriting parts of the application so that it would work on the Macintosh, one programmer was implementing keyboard-driven menus, a capability many business users were asking for that the Macintosh operating system didn't offer. Macintosh users were required to use the mouse. Since there was no Macintosh standard for keyboard-driven menus to follow, the programmer implemented Windows-style keyboard-driven menus to minimize the user interface differences between the Windows and Macintosh versions of the product. When the programmer finished the feature, he called me into his office to demonstrate his new creation. The menus looked just as they did in Windows. I was impressed.

"Wow!" I said as I played with the menus. When the excitement wore off, I turned to the programmer: "How do I disable the Windows interface?"

"Why would you want to do that?" he said, puzzled. "The feature doesn't interfere with the Macintosh mouse-driven interface. There's no reason to disable the interface."

I was surprised by the programmer's response because, at the time, you couldn't pick up a Macintosh-oriented magazine that wasn't full of hatred for Windows. Macintosh users were upset that the industry was raving about Windows, which they considered a third-rate product, and that their beloved Macintosh was viewed as a whimsical toy. Windows was the archvillain to Macintosh users everywhere.

"If Excel ships with Windows-style menus as the default," I said, "it'll alienate Macintosh users. Excel will get killed in reviews if it has 'Windows' written all over it."

The programmer was reluctant to change his code—he'd been thinking he was done and was eager to move on to the next feature. We called over some other team members to talk about the interface. The consensus was unanimous: Excel for the Macintosh not only had to look like a Macintosh product right out of the box but had to bleed Apple's six colors as well. The programmer went back to work.

A while later the programmer emerged from his office, offering to demonstrate his new version of the feature. I was surprised to see that he hadn't merely added an on/off switch for Windows-style menus. He had implemented a smart feature in which the menus were drawn in standard Macintosh format by default but were redrawn as Windows-style menus the moment the user hit the lead-in key for keyboard-driven menus. The menus remained in Windows mode until they were dismissed; then reverted to Macintosh-style menus. Even better, the programmer responsible for implementing the new Macintosh dialogs carried the feature into that code as well. When you invoked a dialog using the mouse, you got a standard Macintosh dialog; when you invoked a dialog by means of a Windows-style menu, the dialog came up with the Windows-style interface. The best of both worlds.

———◆———

Be sure that programmers always view
the product as an end user would.
Programmers must be sensitive to the
end user's perceptions.

———◆———

THE WHOLE PRODUCT AND NOTHING BUT

For the longest time, Microsoft's Languages division—the division responsible for compilers, debuggers, linkers, and so on—viewed the tools as separate, autonomous products. That made sense from a development viewpoint, but it didn't make sense from an end user viewpoint. Programmers who bought a Microsoft development system didn't care whether the compiler and debugger development teams were different. From their viewpoint, Microsoft C/C++, the debugger, and the linker were parts of the same product. Pretty easy to understand.

Unfortunately, that wasn't the predominant attitude toward the tools in the Languages division. Programmers, both external and internal, were asking for improved debugging features, but the debugging team didn't have enough people to fill the requests. Meanwhile, the compiler team was merrily working on code optimizations that few people were asking for. The mindset was "We've got to keep improving the compiler." It should have been "We've got to improve the overall product."

For years, Microsoft's linker was clunky, slow, and tedious to use while competing products had fast linkers. Every programmer in the company knew that Microsoft's linker crawled, but very little was done to improve it. The one programmer assigned to the linker did his best to improve the tool, but he had other duties and didn't have time to make major speed improvements to the linker. Besides, the view in the Languages division seemed to be, it was the compiler that was important—the linker was just a support tool. Users didn't see it that way, though, because they didn't distinguish between the compiler and the linker. To users, they were part of the same product.

At least one Microsoft team dumped the company's own linker and used a competitor's linker. And in the Applications division, a programmer finally got so frustrated with the linker that he hacked together a quick and dirty incremental linker for the Applications teams to use. The Languages group eventually discovered the Applications incremental linker, cleaned it up a bit, and began shipping that linker with retail releases of the compiler.

Eventually, after a few rounds of management change, the Languages group caught on and began improving the *development system*, not just the compiler. The result was Visual C++, a product that reviewers hailed as a refreshing, long-needed change to Microsoft's development system.

*The product is everything that
goes into the box.*

DOUBLE MEANS TROUBLE

As the Excel programmer was writing his keyboard-driven menu code, a Word programmer not more than ten doors away was implementing the same feature in Word for the Macintosh. Although I pointed out this duplicate effort to the Excel programmer and mentioned it to the manager in charge of both Excel and Word, nothing happened. The two programmers continued to implement the code in parallel. When the products eventually shipped, both sported keyboard-driven menus, but the user interfaces were totally different. I saw that as a lost opportunity to make the Excel and Word interfaces work identically, to save half the development effort, and to create a menu library that Microsoft's other Macintosh teams could have popped into their products. The attitude wasn't so much "not invented here" as it was indifference. Nobody seemed to be concerned that programmers were duplicating effort and creating unnecessary differences between products.

I take the other approach to development effort: if I can reuse code that has already been written and debugged, I'll grab it in an instant. Similarly, I always write code assuming that some other team is going to borrow it in the future. No, I don't write all my code so that it's portable, nor do I spend extra time just in case the code might be reused. But if I'm faced with the choice between two equally good designs, I always choose the design that can be more easily shared.

In Excel's initial release, one of the programmers implemented a feature never seen in a Macintosh application before: a "print preview" feature that enabled the user to view pages on the screen formatted as they'd actually be printed. The design for the print preview feature was straightforward. The "page viewer" would take a "picture" of a page and then display it. If the user wanted to preview a full document, another piece of code simply called the viewer to display pictures of successive pages.

The feature was such a hit with users that the Macintosh Word team added a print preview feature to their application, one with a much nicer and more useful page viewer. The Word implementation made Excel's look rough and unpolished. I was assigned the task of adding many of Word's bells and whistles to the Excel version.

My first thought was to scrap the Excel print preview code and transplant Word's implementation into Excel. Not only would transplanting take less time than implementing all the new code, I thought, but transplanting the code would make the two applications look and behave identically. When I explained to the Word programmer what I intended to do, he told me that his implementation of the print preview feature was inextricably tied to Word. He could have written the code to be more shareable, he said, but it had never occurred to him that we might want the code for the Excel project. After all, Excel already had a print preview feature. Sadly, I couldn't use his polished page viewer.

In the end, I enhanced Excel's existing print preview code, but the Word feature was still much nicer. Even more disappointing, because Excel's code was shareable, its version of print preview was the version that spread to Microsoft's other applications.

As I've said, one of the best ways to implement a solid new feature is to grab it from a team that has already done the work of writing and debugging the code. Most programmers appreciate this point. But most programmers, it seems, fail to recognize that they can't grab code unless they and other programmers write their own code so that it *can* be grabbed.

To increase the value of their code to the company, programmers should develop the attitude that all of their code is likely to be reused. With that objective in mind, they should reduce the code's dependence on the host application. It's a problem not unlike writing code to avoid explicit references to global data: sometimes it's necessary, but often by using a slightly different design you can eliminate the explicit dependence with little or no extra effort.

Programmers should ask,

Could this code be useful to other (even future) applications?

If the answer is Yes, the code is a candidate for reuse. Both the keyboard-driven menus and the print preview feature could have been coded in an application-independent way. Reusability just wasn't considered a priority. Too bad. It could have increased the quality of both Word and Excel, with *half* the effort.

———◆———

Give some priority to writing easily shared code. Programmers can't share each other's code unless they're writing it so that it can *be shared.*

———◆———

LEVERAGE YOUR LEVERAGEABILITY

If your team or company is to become successful, you have to ensure that people understand the power of leverage, how a little well-placed effort can yield a much greater return. Every team member should keep this fundamental principle in mind:

You can extract extra value from every task you do by either using existing leverage or creating new leverage.

The one example of this principle that all programmers know about is reusing existing code or creating reusable code. But there are many ways to use or create leverage.

In Chapter 6, I described how you could make employees more valuable to the company by first teaching them skills they could use not just on your project, but on any project. That's creating leverage. As far as your project is concerned, the order in which you teach worthwhile skills doesn't matter. The order in which you teach skills is unimportant until a programmer moves to a new group. Then either the programmer must start at square one because the skills he or she has learned so far are worthless to the new group, or the programmer can leverage the skills learned on the previous project because those skills are more globally useful.

As I've said, you can create leverage out of almost any task—you just need to look for it and then exploit it. For example, during one of the feature reviews for the user interface library, the technical lead handed me his list of proposed library extensions. The functionality looked good—it reflected what the other teams were asking for.

"This looks good," I told him. "But some of these interfaces seem to differ from the way Windows does the same thing. Have you cross-checked the functionality with the Windows reference manuals?"

The lead blew up. "Steve, this library *isn't Windows*. Who cares how Windows does it as long as we provide the functionality in an intelligent way? It seems like a waste to keep pulling out the Windows manuals."

He had a good point. I realized then that I had never explained to him why I felt it was important to model Windows.

"Just so I'm sure I understand," I said, "you're saying that it doesn't matter what our interfaces look like as long as they do their job well. They could mirror Windows interfaces or be totally different. The choice is arbitrary."

"Yeah," he nodded.

"Let me ask you a question. Since Word for MS-DOS uses our library, could a Windows programmer mistake Word's source code for a Windows application if he or she didn't examine it closely?"

"Yeah, but it's *not* Windows code."

"Bear with me," I said. "More than 20 projects use our library. Do you think the programmers working on those projects will stay on those teams forever?"

"No. They'll probably switch to Windows projects."

"I think so too. So tell me, when those programmers switch to Windows projects, how easily will they pick up Windows programming?"

"Pretty easily since our library is like a subset of Windows." You could see the realization sweep across his face even as he said that.

"You mean, we're teaching them Windows programming?"

"And what does it cost the company?"

He thought a moment.

"Practically nothing, I guess—just my having to occasionally look up some functions in the Windows reference manuals."

"Right. And here's something else to think about: How will this Windows experience help *you* in the future? Will you be on this project forever, or will you also eventually move to a Windows project?"

It might seem that you couldn't get leverage out of something as simple as what you name your functions, but you can.

People don't often create new leverage because it calls for looking into the future and making the grand leap of faith, believing that if you create the leverage now, it will actually be used in the future. Will the leverage be used? Maybe not. But the business environment changes so quickly that, to be healthy, a company should create opportunities that can be exploited at a moment's notice. One truth I've seen proven over and over again is this:

> *If you create leverage and make others aware of it, they will someday exploit that leverage.*

When I started the Macintosh cross development project, both the Applications division and the Languages division viewed the work as an in-house-only development system. My goal was to create a development system as an extension of the commercial 80x86 product so that the in-house Macintosh development system could continually inherit all improvements made to the commercial product. That's an obvious case of creating and using leverage, but I pushed for more. I believed that other, non-Microsoft, programmers who were writing applications for Windows would cross-compile those applications for the Macintosh if they had a good—and familiar—cross development system at their disposal. Most people thought I was crazy, but so what? I knew that if we assumed that the cross development system would never be a product, we'd make decisions inappropriate for a product. I also knew that if we wrote the code assuming that it would someday be a product, we'd make decisions that reflected that attitude.

In design meetings I would often point out that, yes, a particular design was workable for an in-house solution but that we'd have to rip it out and start over if Microsoft ever chose to ship the code as a product.

"But we're never going to ship this as a product," I'd hear.

"Well, not if we make that assumption," I'd say. "Let's just take a moment to see if there's an equally good design that would work for both the in-house and product solutions."

In most cases, not only did we come up with dual-purpose solutions, but often the designs were better and took less time to implement. The extra up-front thinking forced us to come up with more designs to consider. In a few cases, the only dual-purpose solution we could find looked as if it would take more time to implement than the in-house solution. In such a case, we chose the in-house design that would require the least additional rewriting if Microsoft ever chose to turn the cross development system into a product.

Whenever upper management asked about the state of the project, I would tell them what they wanted to know and always tell them again of our policy of not doing anything that would prevent the company from shipping the code. Upper management's only concern—one I shared—was that we not spend time doing product work that might never be used.

Nobody ever believed that the code would ship as a product, but one day Microsoft announced its "Windows Everywhere" campaign. All of a sudden it had become strategic for Microsoft to provide Windows solutions for non-80x86 platforms. The Macintosh cross development system was declared a product, given higher priority, and assigned more programmers.

———◆———

Extract the most value possible from
every task you do, by either exploiting
existing leverage or creating new leverage.

———◆———

LEVERAGING ATTITUDES

I've been talking about adopting the attitude that you'll exploit leverage whenever and wherever you see the possibility. That idea pervades this chapter even more than I've suggested. Instilling beneficial attitudes in your team is the ultimate use of leverage. With one small change in attitude you can get a tremendous return for the effort, more return than on any other training investment I'm aware of.

Constant, incremental improvement is great, and that alone is often enough to keep you ahead of your competitors, but if you want your teams to pull ahead, you must help them to develop beneficial attitudes that drive *them* to carry on, without supervision. That lead who was irritated because I asked him to refer to the Windows reference manuals never referred to the manuals himself until I explained the thinking behind my request. Once he understood my motivation—trying to create leverage—I never again had to pester him to check the Windows manuals. He became self-motivated.

HIGHLIGHTS

◆   Novice programmers must understand how difficult writing bug-free code is. If they have that understanding, they won't so readily assume that their code is bug-free. More experienced programmers must understand that even though writing bug-free code is difficult, it doesn't mean they should give up trying to write such code; it means that they must spend more time testing their code up front, before the code ever reaches the testing group. And because it's so difficult to write bug-free code, and so costly when bugs make it into the master sources, all programmers must use every tool at their disposal to detect and prevent bugs, even if that means adjusting their coding styles to weed out error-prone language idioms.

◆ Watch for the "it's too much work" and "it's too hard" reflex reactions. When you hear somebody object that a task will take too much time or that it will be too hard, ask yourself if the individual first considered whether the task was important and whether it matched the project goals and priorities. If it seems to you that he or she was merely responding reflexively, try to refocus the person on the merits of doing the task so he or she can evaluate the idea freshly and fairly.

◆ A common tendency is for people to think negatively when they're faced with something they haven't tried before. In one form or another, they latch onto the idea that the task is somehow impossible. Try to shake up this habitual response and instead help instill in team members the belief that most tasks *can* be done if only people would take some time to think about them. It's amazing how often you can respond to a "can't" judgment with the question "I realize it can't be done, but if it *could* be done, how would you do it?" and hear people rattle off exactly how they would do the thing they just said was impossible. The word "could" takes them out of reaction mode and puts them into thinking mode, right where they should be.

◆ The attitude that the user is neither demanding nor discerning is a detrimental one. Whenever you hear team members expressing such views, remind them that users—who by definition actually use the product—are at least as concerned about speed and the other aspects of software quality as the programmers who write the code.

◆ Teach programmers to view the product as an end user would. Programmers must recognize that end users view everything that goes into the box as a single product. Users don't care how the individual pieces got into the box, they don't care if the product was built by 27 different teams, they don't care what language the code was written in—they don't care about any of that stuff. These points of information may be important to the company, and to the development teams, but users see only that the product is one item produced by one company. Programmers (and leads) may not work on every piece of the product, but they should be concerned when any piece doesn't meet the quality standards set for the product. When enough people express concern about a substandard piece, that piece will get fixed.

◆   Leverage is the most powerful tool at your disposal for adding value to your team, your project, your company, and even the industry. Take advantage of the principle of leverage by using it whenever you can. Strive to create new leverage in every task you undertake, whether it's writing code that could be shared, training team members in a way that makes them more valuable to the company as a whole and not just valuable for your own team, or taking a seemingly arbitrary decision like what you name a function and turning it into a way to prepare programmers for a future project. Think "leverage" in everything you do.

8

THAT SINKING FEELING

When projects start slipping, the first two actions leads often take are the easy, obvious ones: hire more people, and force the team to work longer hours. These may seem like reasonable responses, but in fact they're probably the worst approaches leads can take to turning around a troubled project.

Imagine a sixteenth century merchant galleon crossing the Atlantic Ocean from the Old World to the New World. When the galleon is far out in the ocean, the first mate notices that the ship is taking on water and alerts the captain. The captain orders members of the crew to bail water, but despite their efforts, the water continues to rise. The captain orders more crew members to bail water—to no avail. Soon the captain has the entire crew bailing water in shifts, but the water continues to rise. . .

Realizing that he has no more sailors to call on, and with the ship continuing to take on water, the captain orders all crew members to bail ever longer hours, their days and nights becoming nothing but bailing water, collapsing from exhaustion, waking up, and going back to bailing. It works. The sailors are not only able to prevent the water from rising, but they're able to make headway, bailing water out faster than it's coming in. The captain is happy. Through his brilliant management of human resources, he has prevented the ship from sinking.

At least for the first week.

Soon the crew members get bone weary and bail less water than they did when they worked in shifts and were well rested. The ship again starts taking on more water than they can bail out. The first mate tries to convince the captain that he must allow the crew members to rest if he wants them to be effective. But because the ship is sinking the captain rejects all talk of giving the crew a break. "We're *sinking*. The crew *must* work long hours," the captain shouts. "*We—are—sinking!*"

The water continues to rise and the ship eventually sinks, taking everybody with her.

Could there have been a better approach to saving that ship than putting all the crew members on the bailing task and then forcing them to work long, hard hours? If you were on a ship that was taking on water, what would you do? I can tell you what I'd do: *I'd search for the leaks.* Wouldn't you?

This is such an obvious point, but why then do so many leads run their projects as if they were sinking ships? When a project starts to slip, many a lead will first throw more people onto the job. If the project continues to slip and the lead can't get more people, he or she will demand that the developers put in longer hours. Just as that ship captain did. The project can be waist-deep in water, but the lead won't stop to look for and fix the leaks. Fortunately for their companies, most project teams can bail water slightly faster than it comes in, and they end up shipping their products, but often not without an enormous amount of misplaced effort.

In Chapter 1, I described a user interface library team that had been working 80-hour weeks for more than a year, with no end in sight. Water was gushing in on that project, but nobody stopped to look for leaks.

The team was fully staffed, and they were working 12-hour days, seven days a week. What more could they do? But as I pointed out in Chapter 1, that team was spending most of its time on work they shouldn't have been doing. They were ignoring what should have been their primary goal: *to provide a library that contains only functionality that is useful to all groups who will use the library.* That was a leak.

In Chapter 3, I talked about a dialog manager team that was working hard to speed up their library for the Word for Windows team. Despite all their hard work, they kept falling short of the quality bar for speed that the Word team had set. Word's swapping hack that kicked out all "unnecessary" code segments was kicking out every byte of the library code, so that physically reloading the code, to say nothing of executing the code, took more time than Word's quality bar allowed. But nobody was looking at load issues. The dialog manager team members were focused on optimizing the code to make it run faster.

And in Chapter 5, I described the Excel team's working 80-hour weeks to meet an unrealistic and demoralizing schedule.

In all of those cases, the need to work long hours should have been a red flag, a clear indication that something, somewhere, was seriously wrong. Unfortunately, many leads take the two obvious steps when projects start to slip their schedules—hiring more people and demanding longer hours—instead of looking for the causes of the schedule slips.

HAVE A LIFE

As I've said, for several years at Microsoft, my job was to take floundering projects and make them functional again. In every case, the team members had been working long hours, seven days a week, in a desperate attempt to catch a ship date that was moving ever further away. Team morale was usually low, and often programmers had come to detest their jobs.

On my first day as the new lead, my initial actions were always to put a stop to the long hours and start looking for the causes of the slipping schedule. I would walk down the halls in the early evening and kick people out. "Get outta here. Go have a life."

Programmers would protest: "I can't leave—I'm behind on this feature."

"That's OK," I'd say. "The entire team has been working insane hours for nearly a year, and all that effort hasn't kept the project from regularly slipping. Working long hours won't bring this project under control. There's something fundamentally wrong here, something we need to find and fix, and continuing to work long hours is not going to help us find the problem. Go home. Get some rest. We'll look for the problem first thing tomorrow."

At first the team members would think I was joking. The message they had been getting—in some cases for more than a year—was work harder, longer hours, and I was telling them to go home while the sun was still out. They thought I was nuts. If the project was slipping so badly now, they thought, what would it look like if they stopped working those long hours?

But over the next few weeks, I'd hit the project with all the strategies I've described in the first seven chapters of this book. I'd put a stop to unnecessary reports and meetings and all other unnecessary interruptions. I'd toss out the existing task-list–driven schedule and replace it with a win-able schedule made up of subproject milestones of the type I've described in Chapter 5, cutting all nonstrategic features in the process. I'd promote attitudes I've presented in Chapter 7, such as the attitude that it's crucial that the team fix bugs the moment they're found. I'd make sure that the project goals were clear and that the programmers understood that one of my goals as a lead was to help create large blocks of time during the day for them to work uninterrupted. I'd do all of the things I've encouraged you to do. A hard month or two later, the team would hit their first milestone, as planned, but they'd do it without working 80-hour weeks. They'd have their first win. In the following months, hitting those subproject milestones would get progressively easier as new work skills became habits.

———◆———

If your project is slipping, something
is wrong. Don't ignore the causes
and demand long hours of the team
members. Find and fix the problems.

———◆———

The Commitment Myth

Some teams work long hours, not to meet an ever slipping schedule, but because an upper-level manager demands that they work 80-hour weeks, believing that development teams must work long hours to get products out the door. When such a manager sees a team working 40-hour weeks, his or her immediate interpretation is that the team is not committed to the company. If you point out that the team hits all its drop dates, the upper-level manager will counter with the statement that the team must be padding its schedules with gobs of free time. That same manager will hold up a team whose members work 80-hour weeks as an example for other teams to follow. "This team shows commitment!" If the team isn't hitting its deadlines, well, that's just because the project's schedule is unattainable, just as a schedule should be if you want programmers to work as hard as possible.

Obviously, I disagree with that point of view. If I held that view, I would have to conclude that the user interface library project, the dialog manager project, and the Excel project were model projects to be emulated. And I'd have to conclude that any team who had concrete goals and objectives, who focused on strategic features, who constantly invested in training, and who as a consequence always hit their drop dates while working efficient 40-hour weeks was a team who were screwing up.

It sounds silly when I put it that way, but that's effectively what that manager is saying when he sees a team working only 40-hour weeks and demands that the lead force the team members to put in more hours: "This is *not* a company of clock-watchers. You tell your team they're expected to put in more hours. I want to see some commitment!"

What nonsense. Managers like that praise the teams who work inefficiently and think the worst of the teams who work well. Compare such a manager with a manager who looks at a 40-hour-per-week team and is grateful that at least one project is running smoothly. That manager asks the team what they're doing to achieve such success and works to get other teams to duplicate that success.

Why such opposite reactions to the same event? In a word, attitudes.

The two upper-level managers respond differently because their primary attitudes about projects that run smoothly are polar opposites: one manager assumes that teams who work only 40-hour weeks and who consistently meet their schedules are doing something *wrong*; the other type of manager assumes those teams are doing something *right*. Either manager could be mistaken in the case of a particular project, but what good does it do to start out assuming the worst of a team?

Just as some leads ask first for long hours instead of looking for the real problem and then solving it, some upper-level managers have glommed onto that same uninventive approach, believing that long hours are good for the project and the corporate culture. Such managers forget that the business purpose of a development team is to contribute value to the company. A team can contribute value in numerous ways: reducing their cost-of-goods and thereby increasing the profit per box shipped, writing shareable code that saves development time, and so on. A manager who demands long hours focuses on one obvious way it might seem that programmers can add value to the company: giving the company all of their waking—and some of their sleeping—time.

It might seem logical that having the programmers work all of those hours would enable them to finish the product sooner. Unfortunately, it doesn't work that way, not in software development. If the company made widgets and managers demanded that workers run the widget-making machines for three extra hours every day, the company would get three hours' worth more of widgets—added value. There's a direct correlation between the number of hours worked and the amount of product produced, a correlation that in my experience doesn't exist in software development.

If upper management pressures programmers to put in 12-hour days, working, say, from 10 o'clock in the morning to 10 o'clock at night,

---

Don't Blame the Programmers

I've been picking on the user interface library and dialog manager projects, but the problems with those projects and with the Excel project were not the programmers. In all of these cases, the programmers were working hard, trying to do their best in a frustrating situation. It's easy to make the mistake of blaming the programmers when a project is slipping and not running smoothly, but if the entire team is in trouble, that indicates a management problem.

the programmers might leave the office three hours later than they would otherwise; but consider what actually goes on during those three extra hours.

Take those twelve hours, and subtract one hour for lunch and another hour for dinner since 10 o'clock is rather late to work without stopping to eat. Factor in the natural tendency of programmers who regularly work 12-hour days to fit other activities into their work schedules, such as taking an hour each day to jog in the park or work out at the health club. That leaves nine of the twelve hours for actual work. And since programmers who work 12-hour days don't feel they have time outside work, they wind up taking care of other personal business at the office. I've seen programmers working through their stacks of unpaid bills, writing checks and licking envelopes. I've seen programmers practicing their piano skills on keyboards they keep in their offices. I've seen programmers playing in the halls with other team members, everything from group juggling to "hall golf."

People who work 12-hour days rarely put in more than the standard eight work hours they'd put in if they worked a normal 9-hour day, such as the traditional 8 to 5 workday. A programmer who works 12-hour days might actually get some work done between 8 o'clock and 10 o'clock at night, making it appear to some managers that long hours do result in added productivity, but those two hours actually just make up for dinner and some of the other personal time the programmer spent earlier in the day.

Sometimes a programmer will actually get more than eight hours of work done when he or she stays late—mainly when driven, being kept awake by thoughts of an elusive bug or a feature that's almost finished. The desire to find a resolution keeps the programmer focused on the problem. But in such a case, the programmer will tend to stay late even without pressure from upper management.

As a lead, one of your jobs is to protect the team members from those upper-level managers who think that forcing team members to work long hours is going to be productive. It won't be easy, but you've got to stand firm and fight such demands, explaining to those upper-level managers why their demands will only hurt the project. When upper-level management demands long hours of teams, it's a lose-lose situation for the lead: you have to either fight management or hurt the team. Personally, I'd rather fight upper-level management than force team members to do something I'm fundamentally opposed to, but thankfully, I haven't had to fight many of those battles. Most of the upper-level managers I've worked for at Microsoft and elsewhere have understood that demanding long hours of the team was a misguided and inefficient approach to increasing productivity.

———◆———

Beware of the misguided belief that
long hours result in greater productivity.
If anything, long hours only hurt
productivity.

———◆———

But Successful People Work Their Guts Out

You've probably run across the argument that because extremely successful people, as a group, worked a punishing schedule every day before they "made it," it's clearly necessary to work long hours if you want to succeed.

If you dig deeper, you'll find that extremely successful people didn't become successful because they worked long hours. They became successful because they had an intense inner desire to accomplish something they had envisioned. They worked tenaciously toward their goals because of that inner drive, and it was their constant focus that made them successful. These successful people worked long hours because every fiber of their being drove them to work toward their goals; they didn't work all those hours because somebody else forced them to. There are countless examples of people who put enormous efforts into their businesses or other endeavors and who still did not succeed. Long hours is not the key ingredient. The key ingredients of success are a crystal-clear goal, a realistic attack plan to achieve that goal, and consistent, daily action to reach that goal.

WEEKEND WARRIORS

You can probably get those demanding managers to see that forcing the team to work long days won't increase productivity, that it's better to enable the development team to work more efficiently. But those upper-level managers may turn your argument against you: "You say your team can work efficiently without working long days. Fine. But I want them in here on the weekends. You can't tell me that having them work weekends won't increase productivity." In most cases, they would be right, at least for a while, particularly if the team already works efficient 40-hour weeks and has plenty of personal time in the evenings.

But those upper-level managers need to realize that if they demand that teams work weekends, they may create an adversarial relationship between the teams and management. The people on the development teams know that weekends properly belong to them, not to the company, and the more weekends they're forced to work, the more likely they're going to resent being taken advantage of. If programmers start leaving the team, or worse, the company, to work for less exploitative management, the company loses because those programmers will have to be replaced by new programmers who naturally will know less about the project and might be less experienced overall. The resulting loss of productivity might be great enough to cancel the gains made during all those weekends. And imagine the loss to a team—and this has been known to happen—when a fourth of its members leave the week after their product is released. Does that bother those short-sighted managers? No way: "Good. We've weeded out the wimps and the whiners."

One argument I've heard is that competition is so fierce in the software industry that if a company is to stay competitive, the development teams have to work long hours and weekends. *Have to* is another one of those expressions you should become sensitized to. Saying that developers *have to* work weekends to beat the competition is just another way of saying "We *can't* beat the competition unless programmers work weekends." Oh? The team isn't smart enough to find other ways to release a product earlier? I hope this book brings home the point that there are numerous ways to get the job done with much less effort than most teams are expending.

---◆---

*Weekends belong to the team members,
not to the company. Teams don't
need to work weekends in order to
beat the competition.*

---◆---

THE INITIATION PROCESS

Some people insist that teams must work long hours for an altogether different reason than getting more work done: the practice is vital to team-building, they say. They say that working long hours is an initiation, akin to boot camp, that wears programmers down and ultimately makes them feel that they've earned the right to be part of the team.

Let's assume that the point is true, that some sort of rigorous initiation is beneficial to team-building. Is working long hours really the best rigorous initiation?

In a field such as programming, where the ability to *think* is critical, why put a premium on working long hours? If there's to be an initiation, shouldn't it be one that forces programmers to exercise their brains, to *think* hard? When new programmers start out, they need to learn to think hard about their designs, to think hard about how to implement their designs cleanly, and to think hard about how to thoroughly and intelligently test their implementations. A new programmer needs to learn that when her code has a bug, she must never guess where it is and try to fix it with a lucky change—she must stop and *think* whether she has systematically tracked the bug all the way to its source. She must learn to think about the bugs she finds to determine whether there are related bugs that haven't shown up yet. She must learn to think about how a bug could have been more easily detected and how it could have been prevented in the first place. She needs to learn right at the outset that she is expected to *read* to keep abreast of the industry and to actively increase her skill levels.

These practices are tough to learn and follow through on. Really tough, because they can't be done mindlessly. Yet they must be mastered at some point. Make mastering these practices the initiation—not working long hours, which has nothing to do with programming well.

*Stress the importance of thinking hard,
not working hard.*

I'll Lose My Bonus!

When I went down the halls kicking programmers out of their offices with "Go have a life," some programmers would protest: "But what about bonuses? If I don't work long hours, I won't get a big bonus at review time."

I would explain that I never base bonuses on how much overtime a programmer works, that in fact I view the need to work overtime as an indication of problems that need to be fixed, not as something to reward a programmer for.

"If you want large bonuses," I'd tell the programmer, "look for methods that will help bring our products to market more quickly and with higher quality. Point out areas in which we're duplicating effort, or where we could leverage code written by another team. If you've got an idea for a new type of testing tool that would automatically detect certain kinds of bugs that we have trouble spotting right now, bring it up. If you know of a commercial tool that will do the same thing, that's even better. If you think of a user interface feature that would be more intuitive to use, great—particularly if the idea would work across the product line."

"And if you want to get large *raises*," I'd continue, "increase your personal value to the company by actively learning new skills and developing good work habits—things that will make you work more effectively. If you want to really shine, develop the habit of *constantly* earning bonuses—look constantly for new ways to bring our products to market more quickly and with higher quality. That habit will earn you large bonuses and large raises."

I want programmers to work *better*, not longer.

Turning the Project Around

If your team is currently working long hours and you decide to put a halt to that backbreaking effort in order to focus on finding the causes of problems and fixing them, you'd better brace yourself. When you first start kicking people out, nobody will get any work done. That can be frightening, but it is an essential part of the turn-around process. Just as people don't naturally have study skills, they don't naturally have skills for working efficiently in a 40-hour week. Such skills must be developed, or relearned. Be prepared to do some immediate training.

When I find a programmer who is having trouble getting his work done in a 40-hour week—and I don't believe it's because the schedule is too ambitious—I ask him to make a list of how he spent his time that day, or the previous day, to get a snapshot of how he uses his time. The programmer would typically create a list similar to this one:

◆ Conducted an interview and wrote feedback for Human Resources

◆ Chatted with a programmer on the CodeView team for 30 minutes

◆ Read the daily drop of the *comp.lang.c* and *comp.lang.c++* news groups

◆ Read *PC Week*

◆ Took a two-hour lunch break to eat and run errands

◆ Reviewed a draft section of the user's manual

◆ Attended another team's status meeting to report on the progress of a feature they want

◆ Played air hockey in the game room for 30 minutes

◆ Read 27 e-mail messages and responded to 15 of them

That's how he would have spent his first seven or eight hours at the office, without having written any code. Am I joking? No. In my experience this is a typical list of activities for a programmer who is used to working 12-hour days.

Of course the programmer wasn't reading *PC Week* every day, but throughout the week he was reading *something* every day—the company newsletter and his subscriptions to *InfoWorld, Microsoft Systems Journal, PC Magazine, Windows Sources,* and *Software Development.* E-mail would be a constant interruption. He would conduct one or two interviews a week, read those *comp.lang* news group drops daily, and regularly take two-hour lunches to run errands.

Flextime, or Do Time?

Microsoft, like many high-tech companies, has a "flextime" policy. You can work any hours you want as long as you get your job done. That's why I would find programmers who had no qualms about playing air hockey for 30 minutes or taking two-hour lunches. You can get fired at stricter companies for taking such liberties, but not at Microsoft—as long as you get your job done.

Flextime can be wonderful. If you have a dentist appointment, you just go. You don't need special clearance from your manager. If your daughter is in a school play, you go. If you happen to be a baseball fan, afternoon home games aren't a problem; you hop in your car and go. Flextime can dramatically improve the quality of life for employees because it allows them to design their work schedules around the needs of their personal lives.

But there is a dark side to flextime, one that the Human Resources folks don't tell you about as they itemize the reasons you should join the company. By definition, flextime means that there are no set working hours, so the primary way to gauge whether a programmer is working is to see whether he or she is knocking out features as scheduled. If you think this through a bit further, you can see that if a programmer starts slipping, the implication will be that he or she is not working enough. Nobody comes right out and says that, of course, but there's no question that you're expected to stay until you've finished. It doesn't matter that you've already put in a full day.

If you see that one of the programmers needs to work long days to do his or her job, that's an indication of a problem. Maybe the programmer chronically abuses flextime, using it to mask a pattern of procrastination throughout the day, or maybe the long hours indicate something more serious. Don't ignore the problem.

For a programmer working 12-hour days, such a schedule makes sense. When else is he going to run errands or read all those magazines? If not during "work hours," when? This is the point missed by those upper-level managers intent on having programmers work long hours. They badger the programmers into working long hours, and the programmers inevitably rearrange their lives to accommodate the longer work schedule.

Once I had the programmer's typical workday down in black and white, I would start asking questions.

"Now that you're leaving at a reasonable hour and not at 10 o'clock at night, do you still need to take two-hour lunches to run errands, or can you handle errands after work? Do you read e-mail in batches a few times a day, or do you let e-mail constantly interrupt you? If keeping regular hours meant you had to read your news groups and magazines at home, would you be willing to make that trade-off? Do these talks you're having with people on other teams concern project-related issues that I should be handling instead of you? . . ."

I'd work with the programmer to create a schedule that would allow him to get his work done during the day and leave at a reasonable time. It's not difficult to work with a programmer to create a win-able daily schedule. It just takes action on the lead's part.

———◆———

*Train the development team to work
effectively during a normal workday. Don't
allow them to work long hours, which serves
only to mask time-wasting activity.*

———◆———

I Can't Work During the Day

Programmers themselves regularly complain that they can't get any work done during the day, and a look at that programmer's work list in the previous section supports that contention. Many of the tasks on that work list seem to be legitimate business items. Programmers have to conduct interviews, read and respond to e-mail, review draft sections of user manuals, and so on.

The problem with such necessary business tasks is that they constantly interrupt the primary job: improving the product. Just as reading each e-mail message the moment it arrives chops the workday into little, unproductive time chunks, so too does the regular stream of necessary business if team members don't have a plan for tackling such tasks efficiently. If they're handling each task the moment it lands on their desks, they'll have a difficult time getting work on the product done.

I've heard a lot of management advice recommending that you finish every task the moment it shows up. Either handle it immediately, or decide that you're *never* going to handle it and dismiss it forever. I agree with that advice because it prevents procrastination and helps people to stay on top of things, but I want to qualify the point. If programmers were to blindly follow that advice, interrupting their design and coding work to handle every distraction as it arrived, they wouldn't get much done on their product unless they worked late into the night, when there are usually far fewer interruptions.

The key idea in the advice is to "handle the task the moment it shows up." You might not think that programmers have any control over when tasks show up, but they do. Consider the e-mail example. If programmers respond to their e-mail at set times, only two or three times a day, they turn those random interruptions into predictable daily tasks. Then they can either respond to their messages (handling them immediately) or delete them (never to be considered again).

Programmers can apply the same principle to the other daily interruptions by turning them into predictable tasks that no longer disrupt their work. They just have to create a schedule describing how they'll work during the day—a plan that gives priority to improving the product, not handling interruptions. Take my daily schedule, for example, one which looks like the schedule shown on the next page.

I dedicate the time before lunch, when I'm freshest, to working solely on the product or the project, depending on whether I'm working primarily as a programmer or as a lead. I rarely answer my phone during those hours, and I certainly don't turn on my e-mail reader because reading and responding to e-mail is perhaps the most disruptive activity of the environments I work in. I try to get three or four solid hours of uninterrupted work completed before I do anything else. I don't read and respond to e-mail for the first time until I get back from lunch.

Work solely on the product/project (for a few hours)
Have lunch
Read and handle e-mail for first time
Work solely on the product/project (for a couple more hours)
Read and handle e-mail for second time
Handle all other tasks that have cropped up
Read and handle e-mail for final time

After I handle the post-lunch e-mail task, I have a second block of time devoted solely to working on the product or the project. If other tasks crop up during the day, I don't look at or think about them—they go right into my pile of tasks to tackle at the end of the day, where I have time scheduled to do them. When I finally get to those tasks, I handle them immediately or never. If for some reason I can't finish a task that day, I don't look at it again until the scheduled time the following day.

The point is that, with such a schedule, e-mail and other common interruptions don't distract me from my primary work. I take care of those tasks, but during the time I have *planned* for them, not when they happen to roll in. My schedule turns unpredictable interruptions into predictable tasks, and it puts those tasks lower in my list of priorities than working on the product—just where they should be.

Unfortunately, too many programmers unknowingly have their priorities reversed: they give e-mail and unforeseen tasks higher priority than improving the product, so at the end of the day, they haven't even begun to work on designs or write code. Instead, they have answered e-mail messages that didn't really need responses or tackled tasks that could have been spread over several days. What choice do they have, then, but to work long hours? If they didn't, they'd never get any product work done.

If you truly believe the project schedule is attainable and yet the programmers find they must work long hours to meet that schedule, you still have problems to find and solve. You should check these possible sources of the trouble:

◆   Programmers are allowing unpredictable interruptions to disrupt their work on the product instead of turning those unpredictable interruptions into predictable tasks.

◆   Programmers are giving interruptions higher priority than the primary task.

The schedule I've laid out works well for me, but I'm sure that for others it would be too restrictive or too *something* for their tastes. I'm sure that for some people the idea of not reading e-mail until after they get back from lunch seems impractical: "I can't do that." If reading and responding to e-mail is an integral part of their primary task, I'd agree with them. But if their primary task is working on the product, I'd urge them to try working for a few hours each day before first turning on their e-mail reader. At the very least, I'd urge them to consider reconfiguring their mailers to call their hosts less frequently and to turn off the notification beep that sounds when new mail arrives. In any case, the members of the development team should have daily schedules that help keep them focused on their primary work.

———◆———

Work with programmers to create daily schedules that turn unpredictable interruptions into predictable tasks. The schedules should give their primary tasks priority over all other work.

———◆———

> ### "Working Solely on the Product" Defined
> When I say "working solely on the product," I don't mean that programmers should lock themselves in their offices and barricade the doors, doing nothing but designing and writing code. Spontaneous discussions in the hall, brainstorming sessions, and code reviews are also part of working solely on the product.

Consumed by Excitement

There are a few cases in which working long hours over the short term makes sense—working the weekend right before a drop to put all the finishing touches on the code, for example, or working hard the week before a COMDEX show to create a killer demonstration. But I stress *short term*. Long hours produce increased productivity for only the first week or two, when the sense of urgency is strongest. If you ask a team to work months of 80-hour weeks, they will work hard initially, but once the sense of urgency wears off, they'll fall into the pattern I described earlier—taking two-hour lunches to run errands, having long chats in the hall, and so on.

The exception to this tendency is when people are so excited about their project that you can't get them to leave. Such projects are truly wonderful because you eat, breathe, and sleep programming. I hope that everybody experiences such a project at least once, but I do have one reservation about such projects.

Early in my career, I spent nearly five years working on a handful of projects that were so exciting that I did little but write code, eat, and sleep. So did the other members of the development team. We didn't know what a social life was. We lived to code, often working until 2 or 3 o'clock in the morning, only to return six or seven hours later to start another day. And we loved it. We had that burning desire to see the product finished as we envisioned it.

After working on those projects, I worked on several more exhilarating projects, but I didn't program to the exclusion of all else. I worked a traditional 8-hour day, which gave me the opportunity to pursue an active social life after work—going to parties, taking 40-mile bike rides with friends, going to the theater, learning to ski, meeting new and interesting people. . .

What an eye-opener. If somebody had told me as I worked on those earlier projects to the exclusion of all else that I was missing out on an important part of life—a personal life—I would have laughed at them, just as people using 8-MHz IBM PC machines often laugh at people who suggest they should upgrade to the latest machines, which are 100 times faster. "I'm happy now. Why should I change?" But once the user's machine breaks and she buys a new one, her attitude undergoes a dramatic transformation: "I can't believe I waited so long to upgrade. To think that I was actually *satisfied* with that old clunker!"

Like such computer users, I had no idea what I was missing out on, not having had an active social life for so long. Those projects were so exciting that I never felt the need for a social life; my life was complete as it was. But once I'd worked on exhilarating projects during which I also pursued an active social life, I learned how important it is to have a balanced life. And that has been the driving force behind my desire to do absolutely the best I can in a regular 8-hour day, so that I can balance that work with my personal life, getting the best of both worlds.

As exciting as it was when I was working on those all-consuming projects, I wish that somebody had pulled me aside back then to explain that there was more to life than work. I might not have listened, but I still wish that somebody had tried. So even though programmers on my teams are sometimes so thrilled with their work that they want to work long hours, I urge them, "Go home. Have a life."

Highlights

◆   The need to work long hours is a clear indication that something is wrong in the development process, whether it's because the team is doing nonstrategic work or because the team is being bullied by a misguided manager. No matter what the reason for the need to work long hours, leads must not ignore the problem and continue to let the team work late into the night over the long term. Leads must tackle that problem and make it possible for team members to work effectively in the scheduled 40-hour week.

◆   I often hear upper-level managers and project leads praise team members for working long hours. "Your commitment to the company is admirable. Excellent job!" That's exactly the wrong message that managers and leads should be sending. People should be praised for working well, not for the number of hours they're in the building. Managers and leads must never confuse "productivity" with "time at the office." One person might work far fewer hours and produce more than somebody who works twice as long.

◆ You can minimize meetings, reports, and other corporate processes, but unless you also focus on the wasted effort unique to each individual, you'll be missing a significant part of the problems you need to work on. Make it a priority to help each team member design large blocks of uninterrupted time into his or her daily work schedule.

◆ If you care about your team members, don't allow them to spend all their waking hours at work. Make sure they work a solid 8-hour day, and then kick them out. Taking that stand at your organization may seem sacrilegious, but if you believe, as I do, that people work better if they have an enjoyable personal life, take that stand.

◆ There's nothing sacred about the 40-hour work week. It's a U.S. tradition, so software projects tend to be scheduled on the assumption that each programmer will work a 40-hour week—five 8-hour workdays. If it takes a lot more than 40 hours per week per programmer to meet one of those schedules, something is wrong. The schedule might be unrealistic, or the programmers might need more training. Either way, there is a problem that needs to be fixed—not masked by having the programmers work long hours to compensate for the problem.

Epilogue

A WORD ON LEADING

Occasionally I'll come across the idea that as the lead for a project, you cannot and never will be a part of the team, that you will always be a step removed, and that there is nothing you can do about it. In my experience, that isn't true. I've been a part of dozens of teams—as both lead and programmer—and without exception the teams that jelled were those in which the lead was just another person on the team, one who happened to have some nonprogramming responsibilities. There was never the feeling that the lead was superior.

To someone who didn't know much about American football, the quarterback might seem to be in a superior position with respect to the other players. After all, the quarterback calls each play, the quarterback is the focal team member who has control of the ball, and after a victory it's the quarterback who usually gets carried off the field by the other team members.

The quarterback might appear to be superior in rank to the other players, but we know better. The quarterback is just another team member who happens to have unique responsibilities. An effective project lead is no different. He or she understands that a focal team member is not superior to other team members:

> *The lead is just another team member, who, like every other team member, has his or her own set of unique responsibilities.*

Effective leads understand that team members play different roles on the team. Some team members are responsible for the data entry part of the project, others for the print engine, still others for foreign file converters and the user interface design. Leads may implement features along with everybody else, but in addition to that work, they have the responsibility for setting project goals and priorities, keeping dependent groups such as Testing and Marketing informed of progress, creating an environment in which the team members can work effectively, and ensuring that team members are learning new skills as a way of adding value to the company. A lead can do all those tasks without adopting the attitude that he or she is superior.

If a lead has the attitude that he or she is superior, a whole array of harmful behaviors follows. Here's what happens in extreme cases:

◆ The lead blames the team for failures but gladly takes the credit for successes.

◆ The lead doesn't care about the people on the team. They're just workers. Who cares if they work 80-hour weeks? The lead is concerned only that the team might make him look bad by missing a scheduled date.

◆ The lead expects team members to jump at every command and never question her authority. "I said 'do it,' so *do it*" is the motto.

◆ Anxious not to appear inferior in any way, the lead attacks any team member who threatens his authority or who appears to be more skilled or knowledgeable than the lead in any area.

◆ Because she must always be right, the lead never admits it when she is wrong.

- The lead shuts down anybody who suggests improvements to the development process or otherwise rocks the boat.

- The lead acts as if he is indispensable.

Granted, not all leads who think of themselves as superior behave so tyrannically, but even in mild cases the air of superiority still comes through. Do team members work *for* the lead or *with* the lead? The very language the lead uses reveals the underlying attitude.

A lead who views herself as a team member works better because she spends little or no time fighting to keep the other team members in their place—why should she? By choosing to adopt the attitude that she's not superior, she relieves herself of having to attack perceived threats to her authority. When such a lead discovers a superstar on the team she's just inherited, she doesn't raise her guard and start the territorial one-upmanship battle so common in people who must feel superior. Such a lead is more likely to be thankful and to work together with the superstar for the benefit of the project.

Your own attitude as a lead can influence everything you do. If you and a team member disagree over a performance review, how do you react? Do you stand firm because you feel you need to be "right," or do you discuss the problem to see if there's another valid interpretation of events? If you and the team member still disagreed, would you amend the review to describe both positions so that others who read the review later could make their own evaluations?

Look again at the bulleted list that characterizes the behaviors of the leads who insist on regarding themselves as superior. Would a lead who viewed herself as just another team member exhibit those kinds of behavior? Which type of lead would you be more willing to work with, one who behaves in a superior way or one who treats you with more respect? Be the kind of lead *you* would want to work with.

◆

Leads should see themselves
as members of their teams, not
as superior to them.

◆

REFERENCES

These books are explicitly referenced in the text.

Bentley, Jon. *Writing Efficient Programs*. Englewood Cliffs, N. J.: Prentice Hall, 1982.

DeMarco, Tom, and Timothy Lister. *Peopleware: Productive Projects and Teams*. New York: Dorset House, 1987.

Gerber, Michael E. *The E-Myth: Why Most Small Businesses Don't Work and What To Do About It*. New York: Harper Business, 1986.

Kernighan, Brian W., and P. J. Plauger. *The Elements of Programming Style*. 2d ed. New York: McGraw-Hill, 1978.

Koenig, Andrew. *C Traps and Pitfalls*. Reading, Mass.: Addison-Wesley, 1989.

Maguire, Steve. *Writing Solid Code*. Redmond, Wash.: Microsoft Press, 1993.

McConnell, Steve. *Code Complete*. Redmond, Wash.: Microsoft Press, 1993.

McCormack, Mark H. *What They Don't Teach You at Harvard Business School*. New York: Bantam Books, 1984.

Weinberg, Gerald M. *The Psychology of Computer Programming*. New York: Van Nostrand Reinhold, 1971.

These educators are mentioned in the preface:

Anthony Robbins
Robbins Research International, Inc.
9191 Towne Centre Drive, Suite 600
San Diego, CA 92122
Phone: (800) 445-8183
FAX: (619) 535-0861

Michael E. Gerber
Gerber Business Development Corporation
1135 N. McDowell Blvd.
Petaluma, CA 94954
Phone: (707) 778-2900

INDEX

ABOUT THE AUTHOR

Steve Maguire graduated from the University of Arizona with a degree in electrical and computer engineering, but he has always gravitated toward work in computer software. Steve has programmed professionally for the past 19 years in both Japan and the United States. In the late 1970s Steve regularly contributed developer tools, applications utilities, and the occasional video game to the Processor Technology and NorthStar users' groups. Steve has been responsible for numerous projects since then, including *valFORTH* in 1982, an award-winning FORTH development system that enabled Atari programmers to write high-quality graphics applications and video games.

In 1986 Steve joined Microsoft Corporation for the opportunity to work on high-end Macintosh applications. Steve worked on Microsoft Excel and led the development of Microsoft's Intel-hosted MC680x0 Macintosh cross development system. He was the driving force behind Microsoft's switch to a cross-platform shared code strategy in its applications development and is perhaps best known in the company for his efforts to increase the utility and quality of shared code libraries. As a veteran software design engineer and project lead, Steve spent several of his years at Microsoft working with troubled projects—enabling teams to work effectively and, not incidentally, to enjoy their work.

Debugging the Development Process is the second of several books Steve is writing to give programmers practical guidelines for developing professional, high-quality software. His first book, the critically acclaimed *Writing Solid Code* (Microsoft Press, 1993), focuses on strategies that programmers can use to write bug-free programs. It won a prestigious *Software Development* Jolt Productivity Award and awards from the Society for Technical Communication in 1994.

Steve lives in Seattle, Washington, with his wife, Beth, and their Airedale terrier, Abby. He can be reached at *stephenm@stormdev.com* or *microsoft!storm!stephenm.*

The manuscript for this book was prepared
using Microsoft Word 5.0 for the Macintosh
and submitted to Microsoft Press in electronic
form. Galleys were prepared using Microsoft
Word 2.0 for Windows. Pages were composed
by Microsoft Press using Aldus PageMaker
5.0 for Windows, with text and display type
in Palatino. Composed pages were delivered
to the printer as electronic prepress files.

Cover Designer
Rebecca Johnson

Interior Graphic Designer
Kim Eggleston

Principal Compositor/Illustrator
Peggy Herman

Principal Proofreader/Copy Editor
Deborah Long

Indexer
Julie Kawabata

STEVE MAGUIRE'S *WRITING SOLID CODE,* the companion volume to *Debugging the Development Process,* covers techniques and strategies that programmers can use immediately to reduce their bug rates and write bug-free code.

Steve Maguire maintains that the most critical requirement for writing bug-free code is to become attuned to what causes bugs. All of the techniques and strategies Maguire presents in *Writing Solid Code* are the result of programmers asking themselves two questions over and over, year after year, every time they find a bug in their code:

◆ How could I have *automatically* detected this bug?

◆ How could I have *prevented* this bug?

The easy answer to both questions would be "better testing," but that's not automatic, nor is it really preventive. Maguire says that answers like "better testing" are so general they have no muscle—they're effectively worthless. He insists that good answers to the two questions result in the specific techniques that will eliminate the kind of bug you've just found.

Writing Solid Code is devoted to the techniques and strategies that have been found to reduce or completely eliminate entire classes of bugs. Some of the book's points smack right up against common coding practices, but all have been effective in reducing the number of bugs in code. The book also covers techniques that programmers can use to automatically detect bugs—techniques other than using test applications. By building "debug code" directly into their programs, code that monitors a program from the inside, programmers can automatically detect numerous types of otherwise hard-to-find bugs. *Writing Solid Code* covers the most effective ways to write such debug code.

The book is written in the same format and style as *Debugging the Development Process.* Its examples are written in the C programming language, but its good advice is generally applicable—regardless of whether you're using C, FORTRAN, or some other programming language. The next few pages contain an excerpt from *Writing Solid Code*'s Chapter 5, "Candy-Machine Interfaces."

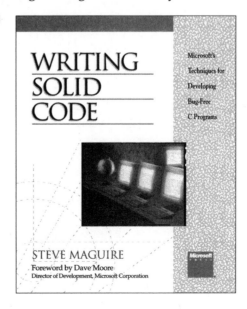

WRITING
SOLID
CODE

Microsoft's
Techniques for
Developing
Bug-Free
C Programs

STEVE MAGUIRE
Foreword by Dave Moore
Director of Development, Microsoft Corporation

Microsoft

HERE'S WHAT THE CRITICS HAVE SAID about the bestselling *Writing Solid Code*, winner of a 1994 *Software Development* Jolt Productivity Award and of awards from the Society for Technical Communication.

Maguire's writing style is fluid and clear, and the content is intended to provoke both thought and action (namely changes in your bad habits).

—Ray Valdés, ***Dr. Dobb's Journal***

This unique volume gathers a wealth of coding wisdom developed over the years inside Microsoft. These aren't coding techniques so much as coding and testing *philosophies*— mindsets that help Microsoft's programmers produce better code with fewer bugs in less time than their competitors.

—Jeff Duntemann, ***PC Techniques***

Writing Solid Code is superbly written and offers a variety of sound practical coding guidelines at a level suitable for the professional C coder. The author's experience, coupled with an obvious enthusiasm for the subject, has resulted in a book which is both informative and easy to read. . . You'll find historical notes about the development of programs such as [Microsoft] Excel and Word. . . You do not, incidentally, need to be an MSDOS, Windows, or Apple Mac programmer to appreciate the wisdom in this book or to follow the code. . . An excellent book and one of those relatively rare offerings that all C programmers would do well to read.

—Paul Overaa, ***Computing***

If you are serious about developing C code, read this book. Consider it carefully. Reject it if you will, but I think you would be foolish to do so. This is easily my 'Book of the Year.'

—*C Vu*

5

CANDY-MACHINE INTERFACES

One of the perks that Microsoft gives its employees is free soft drinks, flavored seltzer water, milk (chocolate too!), and those little cartons of fruit juices. As much as you want. But, darn it, if you want candy, you have to pay for that yourself. Occasionally, I would get the munchies and stroll down to a vending machine. I'd plunk in my quarters, press 4 and then 5 on the selection keypad, and watch in horror as the machine spit out jalapeño-flavored bubble gum instead of the Grandma's Peanut Butter Cookie I thought I'd asked for. Of course, the machine was right and I was wrong—number 45 was the gum. A quick look at the little sign by the cookie would always verify my mistake: No. 21, 45¢.

87

That candy machine always infuriated me because if the engineers had spent an extra 30 seconds thinking about their design, they could have saved me, and I'm sure countless others, from getting something they didn't want. If one of the engineers had thought, "Hmm. People are going to be thinking '45¢' as they deposit their money—I'll bet some of them are going to turn to the keypad and mistakenly enter the price instead of the selection number. To prevent that from happening, we should use an alphabetic keypad instead of a numeric one."

The machine wouldn't have cost any more to make, and the improvement wouldn't have changed the design in any appreciable way, but every time I turned to the keypad to punch in 45¢, I would find I couldn't and so be reminded to punch in the letter code. The interface design would have led people to do the right thing.

When you design function interfaces, you face similar problems. Unfortunately, programmers aren't often trained to think about how other programmers will use their functions, but as with the candy machine, a trivial difference in design can either cause bugs or prevent them. It's not enough that your functions be bug-free; they must also be safe to use.

getchar GETS AN *int*, OF COURSE

Many of the standard C library functions, and thousands of functions patterned after them, have candy-machine interfaces that can trip you up. Think about the *getchar* function, for instance. The interface for *getchar* is risky for several reasons, but the most severe problem is that its design encourages programmers to write buggy code. Look at what Brian Kernighan and Dennis Ritchie have to say about it in *The C Programming Language*:

Consider the code

```
char c;

c = getchar();
if (c == EOF)
    ...
```

On a machine which does not do sign extension, c is always positive because it is a char, yet EOF is negative. As a result, the test always fails. To avoid this, we have been careful to use int instead of char for any variable which holds a value returned by getchar.

With a name such as *getchar* it's natural to define *c* to be a character, and that's why programmers get caught by this bug. But really, is there any reason *getchar* should be so hazardous? It's not doing anything complex; it's simply trying to read a character from a device and returning a possible error condition.

The code below shows another problem common in many function interfaces:

```
/* strdup -- allocate a duplicate of a string. */

char *strdup(char *str)
{
    char *strNew;

    strNew = (char *)malloc(strlen(str)+1);
    strcpy(strNew, str);

    return (strNew);
}
```

This code will work fine until you run out of memory and *malloc* fails, returning *NULL* instead of a pointer to memory. Who knows what *strcpy* will do when the destination pointer, *strNew*, is *NULL*, but whether *strcpy* crashes or quietly trashes memory, the result won't be what the programmer intended.

Programmers have trouble using *getchar* and *malloc* because they can write code that appears to work correctly even though it's flawed. It's not until weeks or months later that the code crashes unexpectedly because, as in the sinking of the *Titanic*, a precise series of improbable events takes place and leads to disaster. Neither *getchar* nor *malloc* leads programmers to write correct code; both lead programmers to ignore the error condition.

The problem with *getchar* and *malloc* is that their return values are imprecise. Sometimes they return the valid data that you expect, but other times they return magic error values.

If *getchar* didn't return the funny *EOF* value, declaring *c* to be a character would be correct and programmers wouldn't run into the bug that Kernighan and Ritchie talk about. Similarly, if *malloc* didn't return *NULL* as though it were a pointer to memory, programmers wouldn't forget to handle the error condition. The problem with these functions is not that they return errors, but that they bury those errors in normal return values where it's easy for programmers to overlook them.

What if you redesigned *getchar* so that it returned both outputs separately? It could return *TRUE* or *FALSE* depending upon whether it successfully read a new character, and the character itself could be returned in a variable that you pass by reference:

```
flag fGetChar(char *pch);      /* prototype */
```

With the interface above, it would be natural to write

```
char ch;

if (fGetChar(&ch))
    ch has the next character;
else
    hit EOF, ch is garbage;
```

The problem with *char* vs. *int* goes away, and it's unlikely that any programmer, no matter how green, would accidentally forget to test the error return value. Compare the return values for *getchar* and *fGetChar*. Do you see that *getchar* emphasizes the character being returned, whereas *fGetChar* emphasizes the error condition? Where do you think the emphasis should be if your goal is to write bug-free code?

True, you do lose the flexibility to write code such as

```
putchar(getchar());
```

but how often are you certain that *getchar* won't fail? In almost all cases, the code above would be wrong.

Some programmers might think, "Sure, *fGetChar* may be a safer interface, but you waste code because you have to pass an extra argument when you call it. And what if a programmer passes *ch* instead of *&ch*? After all, forgetting the *&* is an age-old source of bugs when programmers use the *scanf* function."

Good questions.

Whether the compiler will generate better or worse code is actually compiler dependent, but granted, most compilers will generate slightly more code at each call. Still, the minor difference in code size is probably not worth worrying about when you consider that the cost of disk and memory storage is plummeting while program complexity and associated bug rates are climbing. This gap will only get larger in the future.

The second concern—passing a character to *fGetChar* instead of a pointer to a character—shouldn't worry you if you're using function prototypes as suggested in Chapter 1. If you pass *fGetChar* anything but a pointer to a character, the compiler will automatically generate an error and show you your mistake.

The reality is that combining mutually exclusive outputs into a single return value is a carryover from assembly language, where you have a limited number of machine registers to manipulate and pass data. In that environment, using a single register to return two mutually exclusive values is not only efficient but often necessary. Coding in C is another matter—even though C lets you "get close to the machine," that doesn't mean you should write high-level assembly language.

When you design your function interfaces, choose designs that lead programmers to write correct code *the first time*. Don't use confusing dual-purpose return values—each output should represent exactly one data type. Make it hard to ignore important details by making them explicit in the design.

———◆———

Make it hard to ignore error conditions.
Don't bury error codes in return values.

———◆———

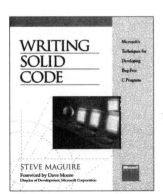

Writing Solid Code
Microsoft's Techniques for Developing Bug-Free C Programs
Steve Maguire

Foreword by Dave Moore
Director of Development, Microsoft Corporation

288 pages, softcover
$24.95 ($32.95 Canada)
ISBN 1-55615-551-4